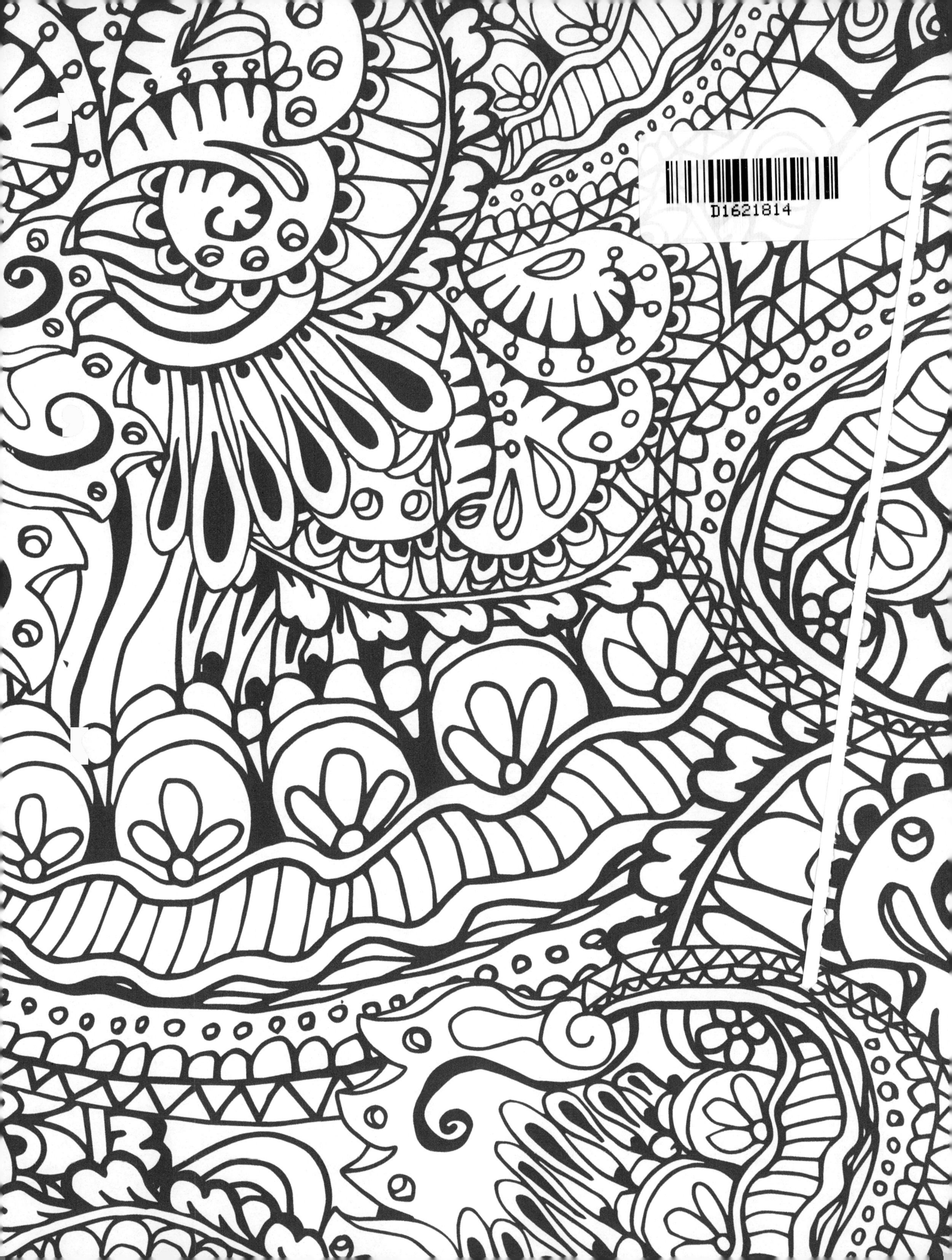

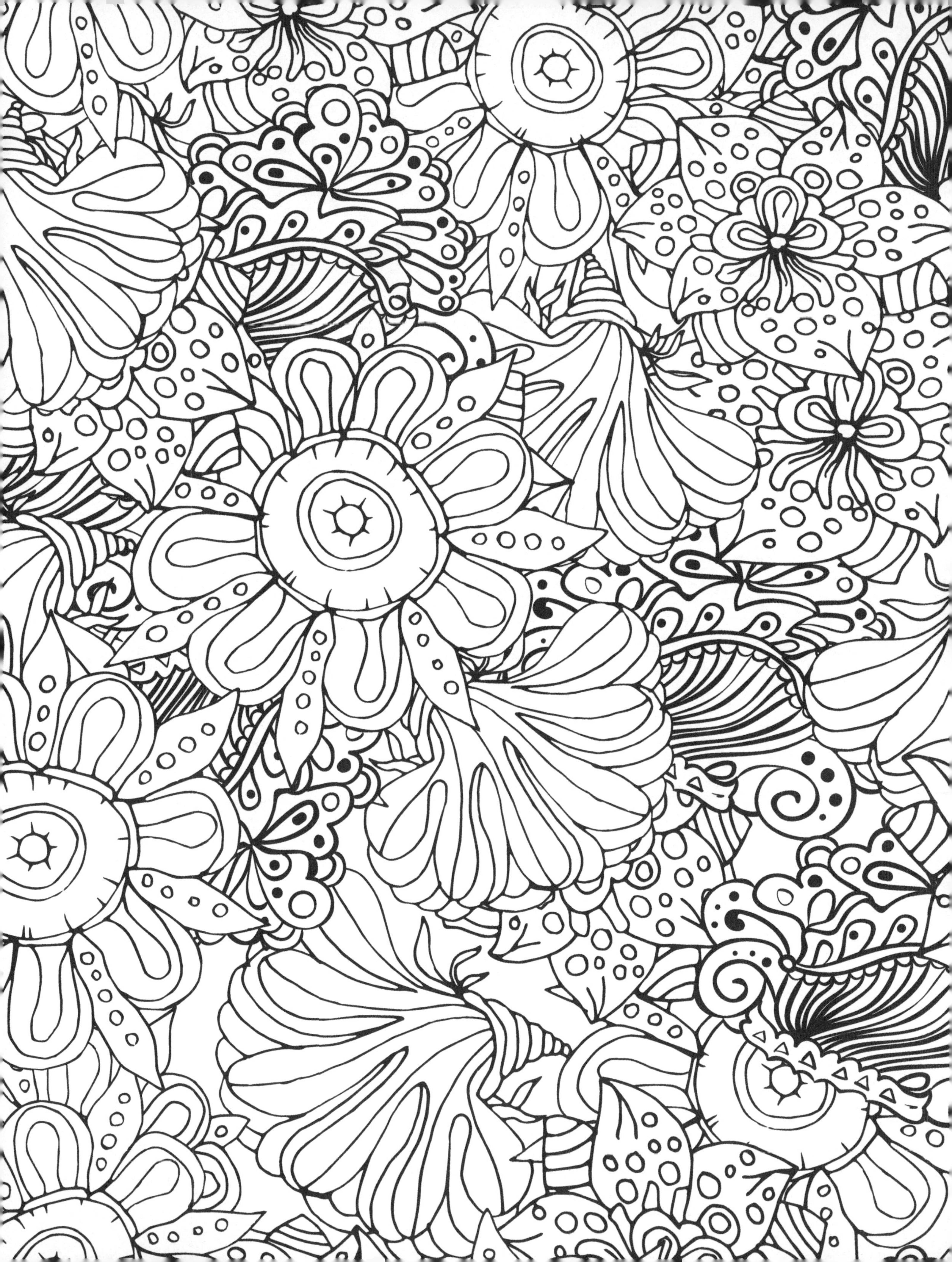

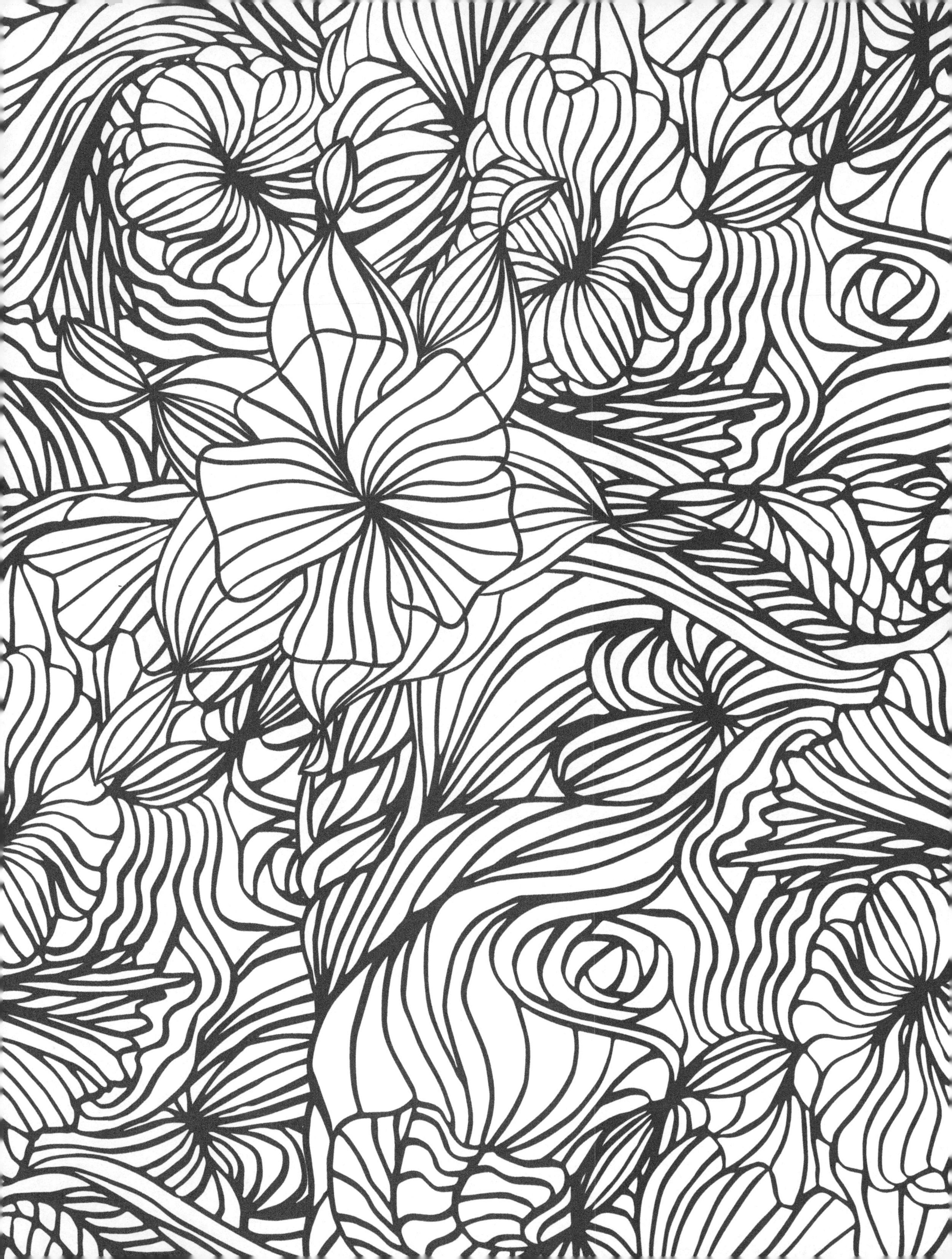

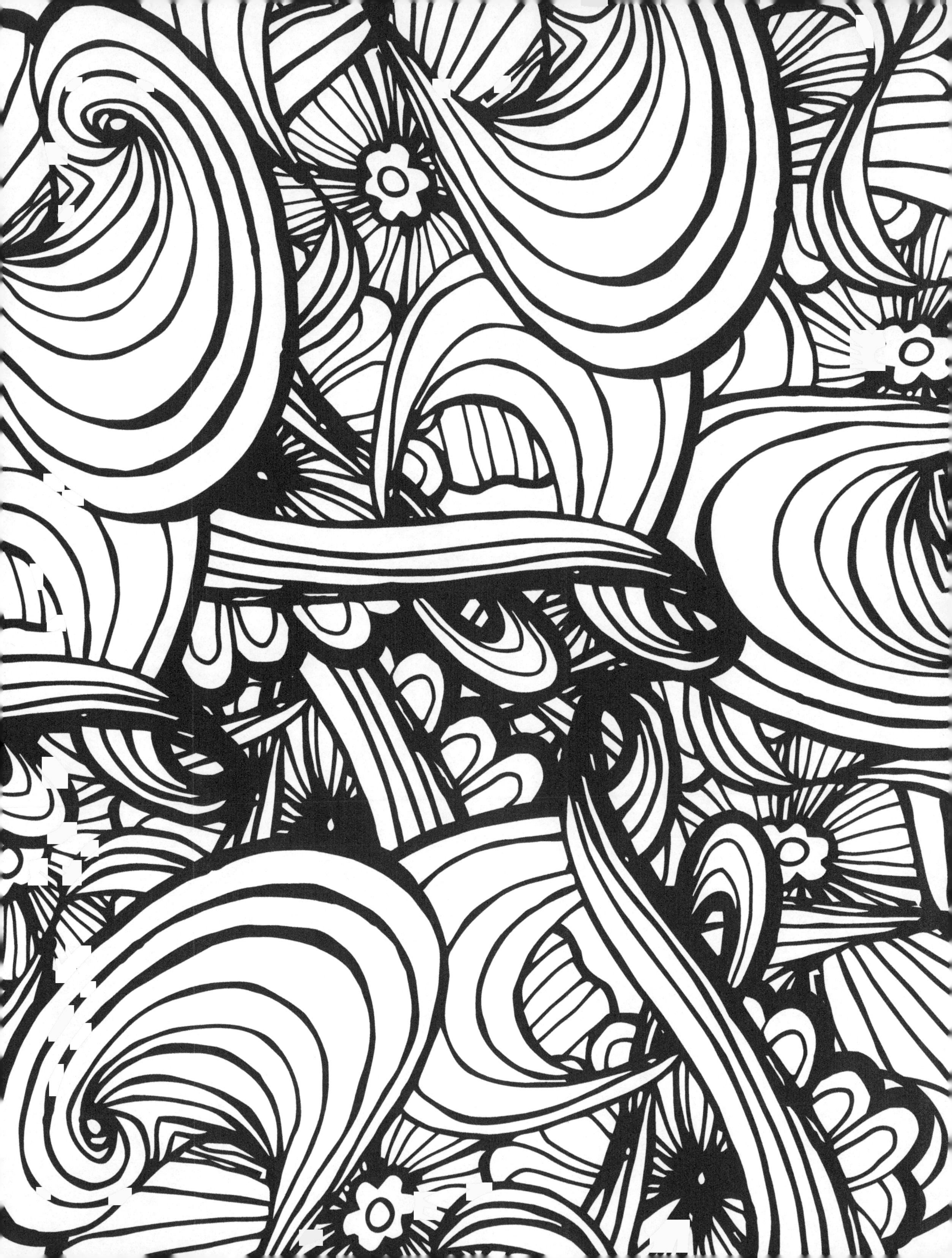

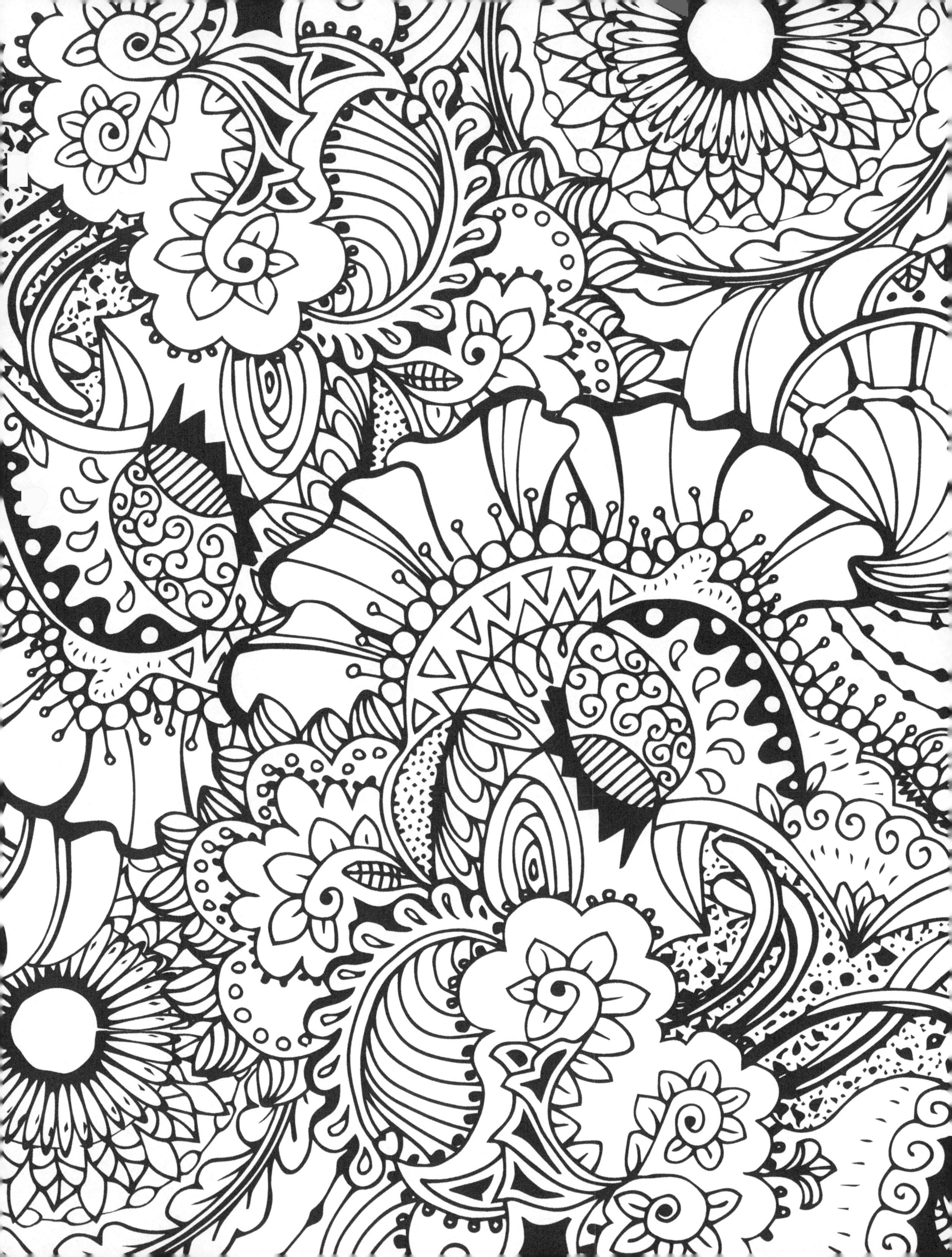

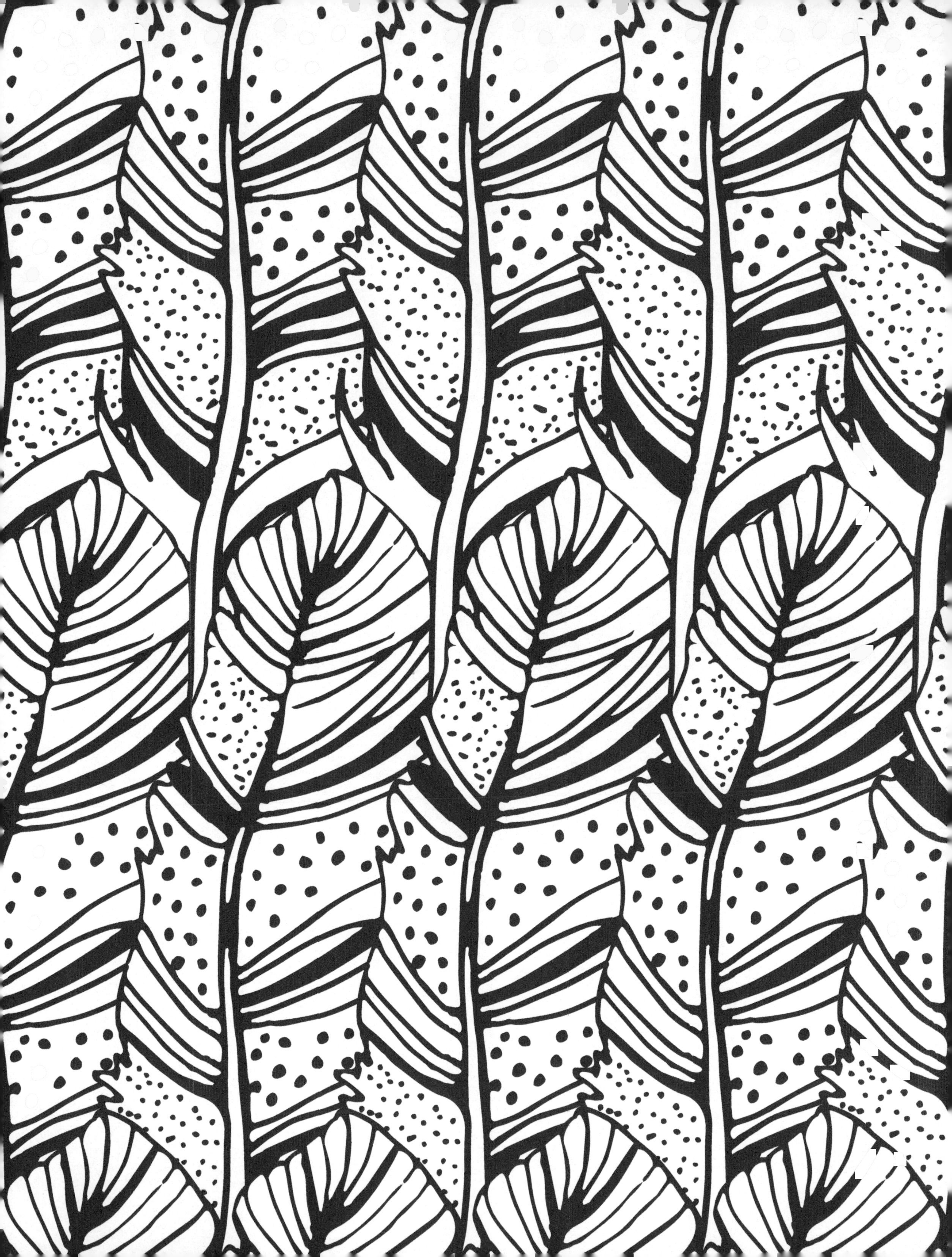

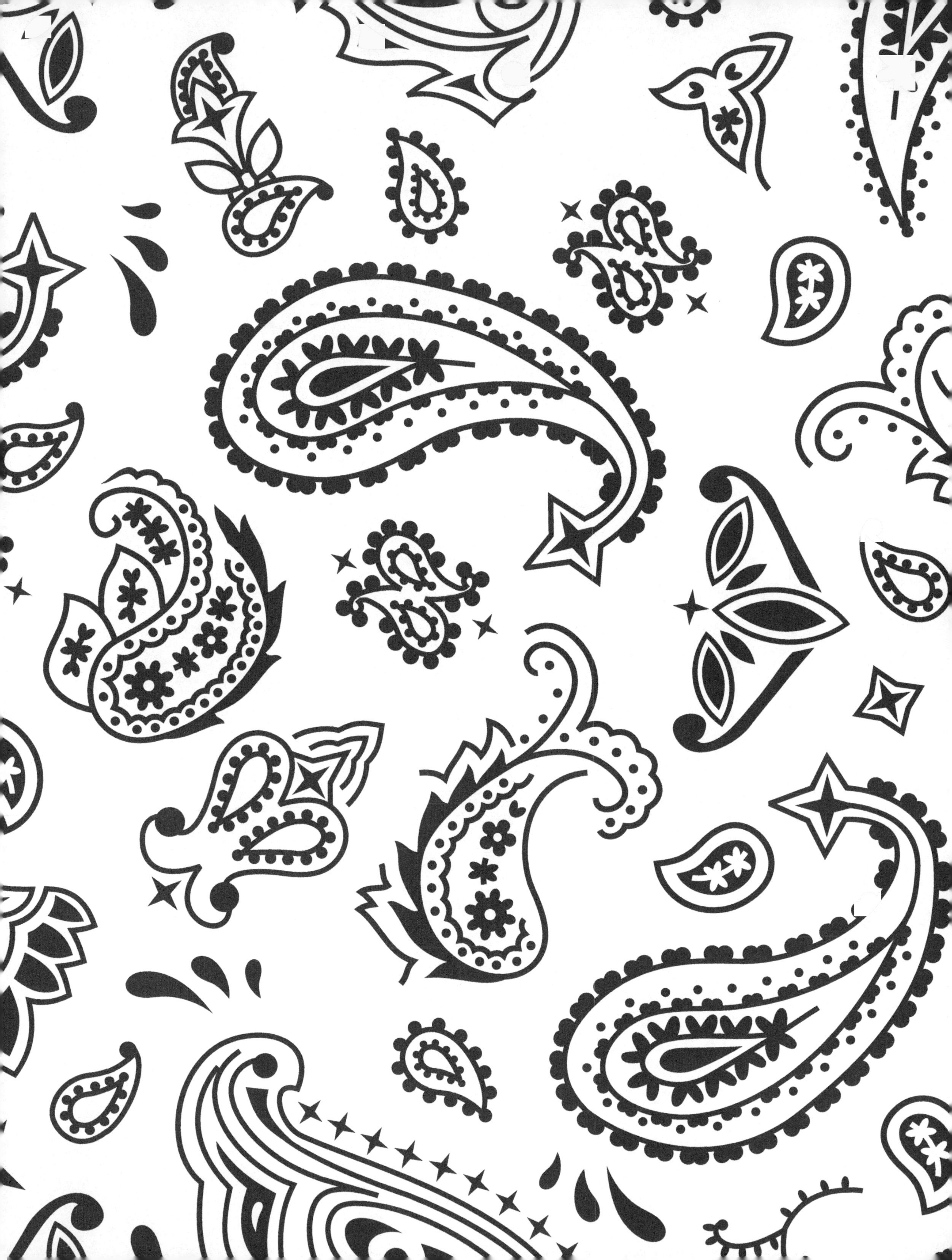

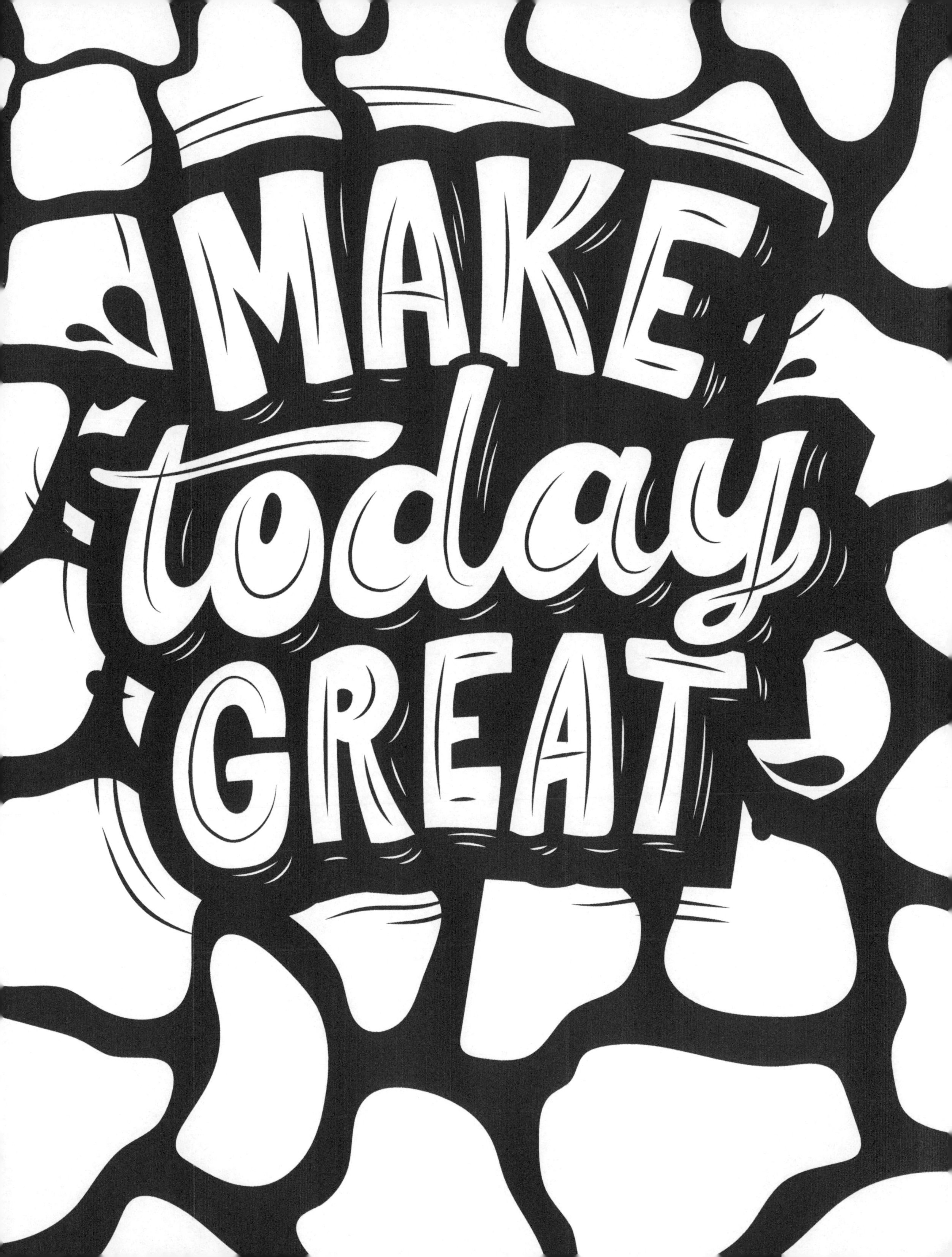
MAKE
today
GREAT

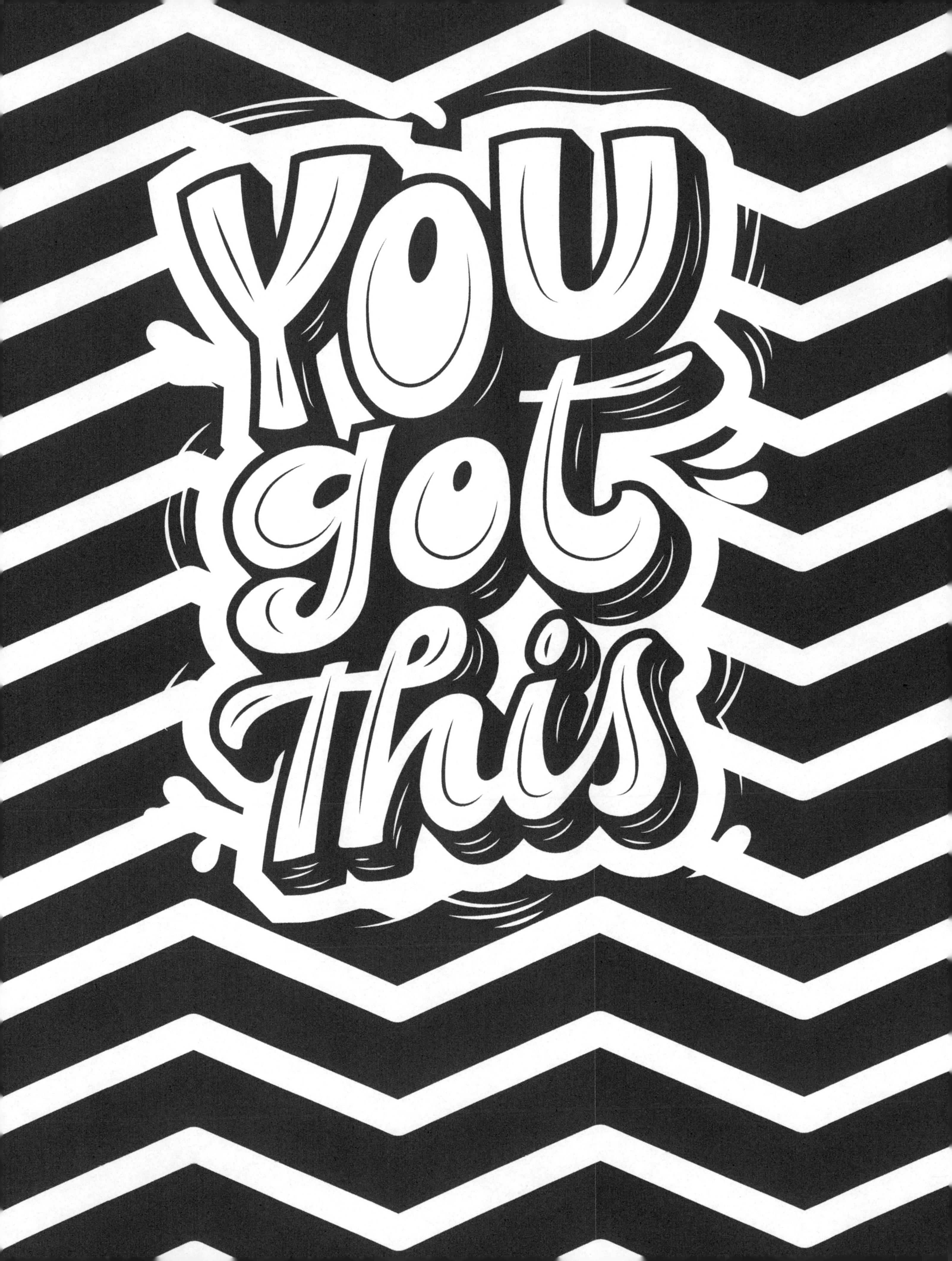
You got this

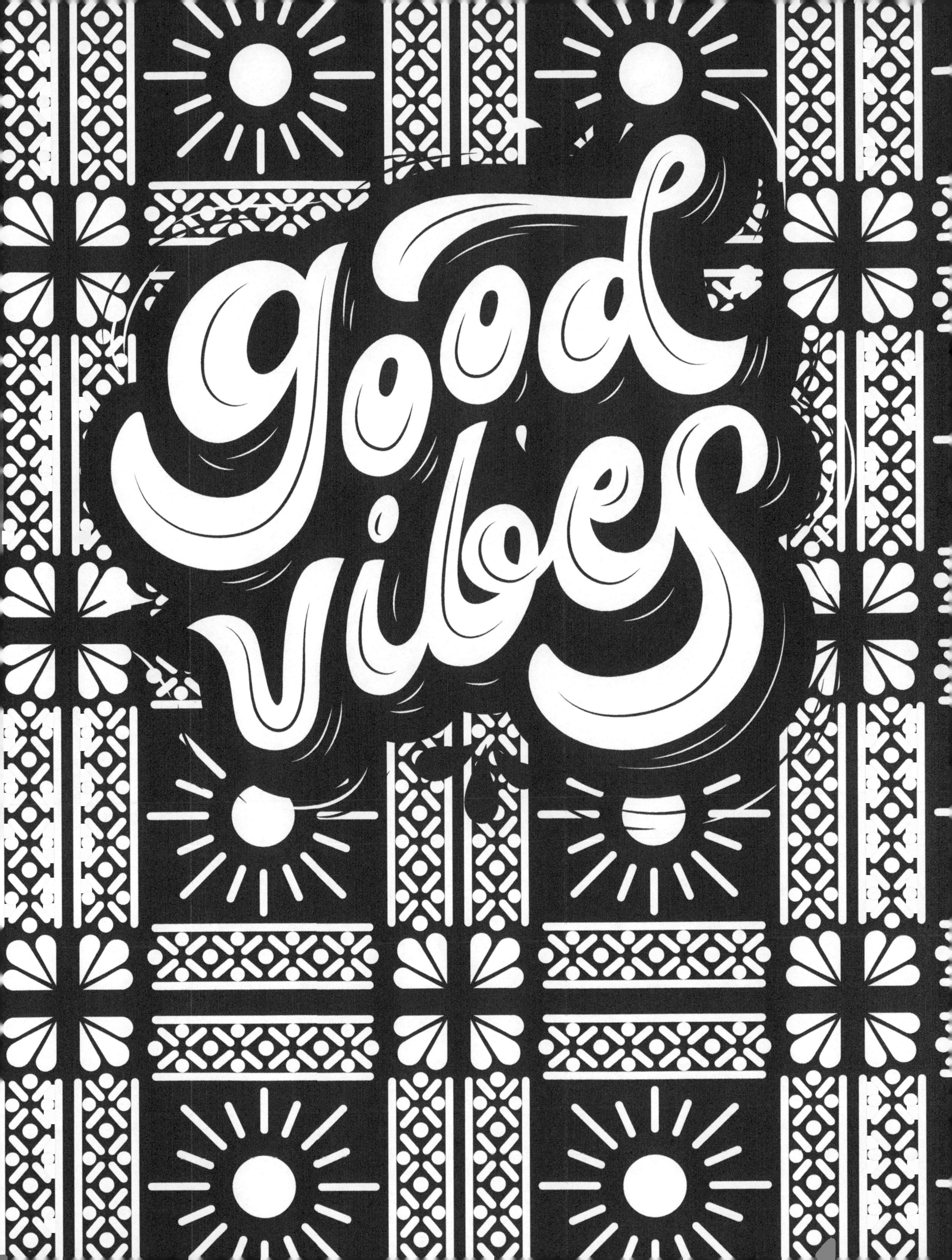
good
vibes

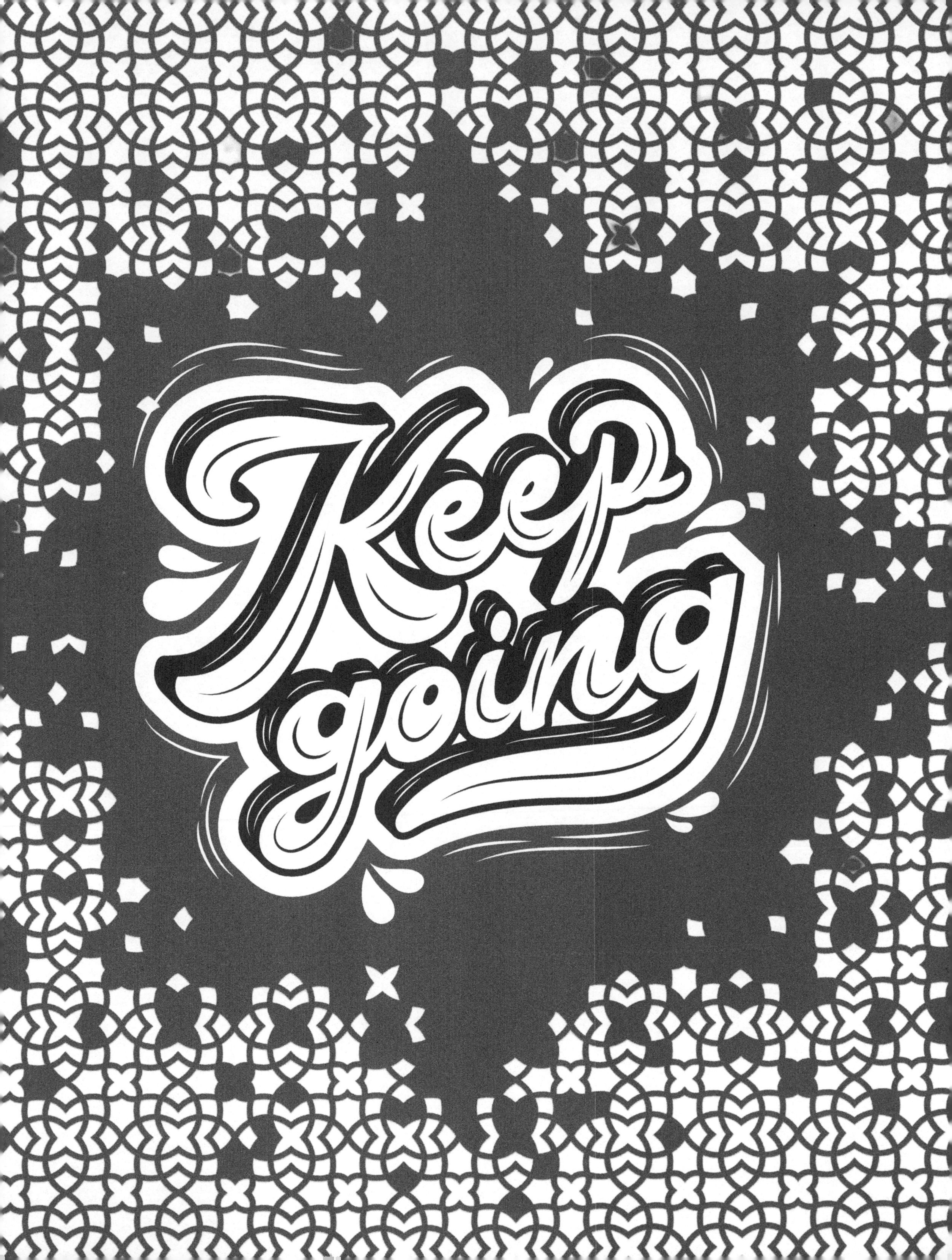
Keep going

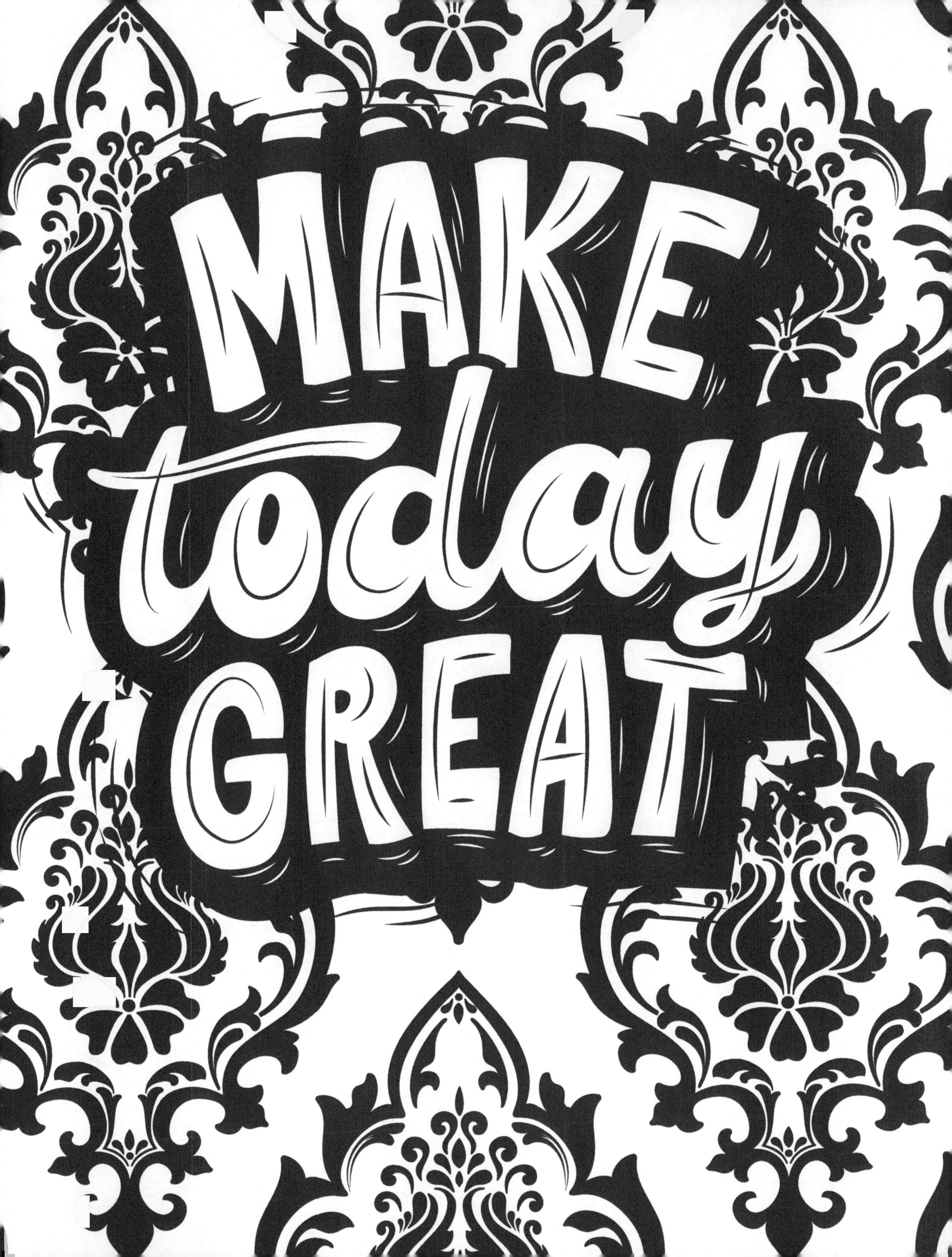
MAKE
today
GREAT

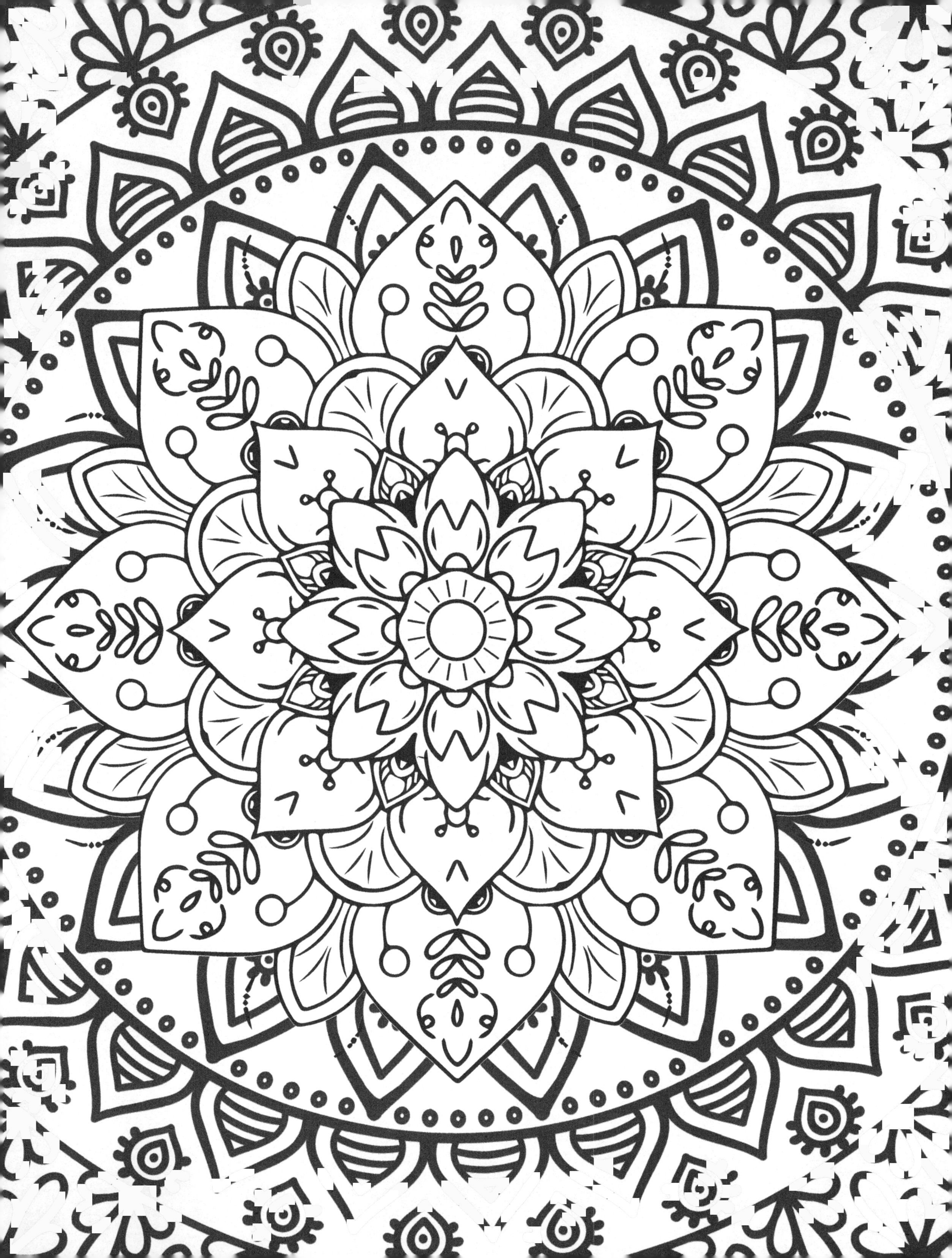

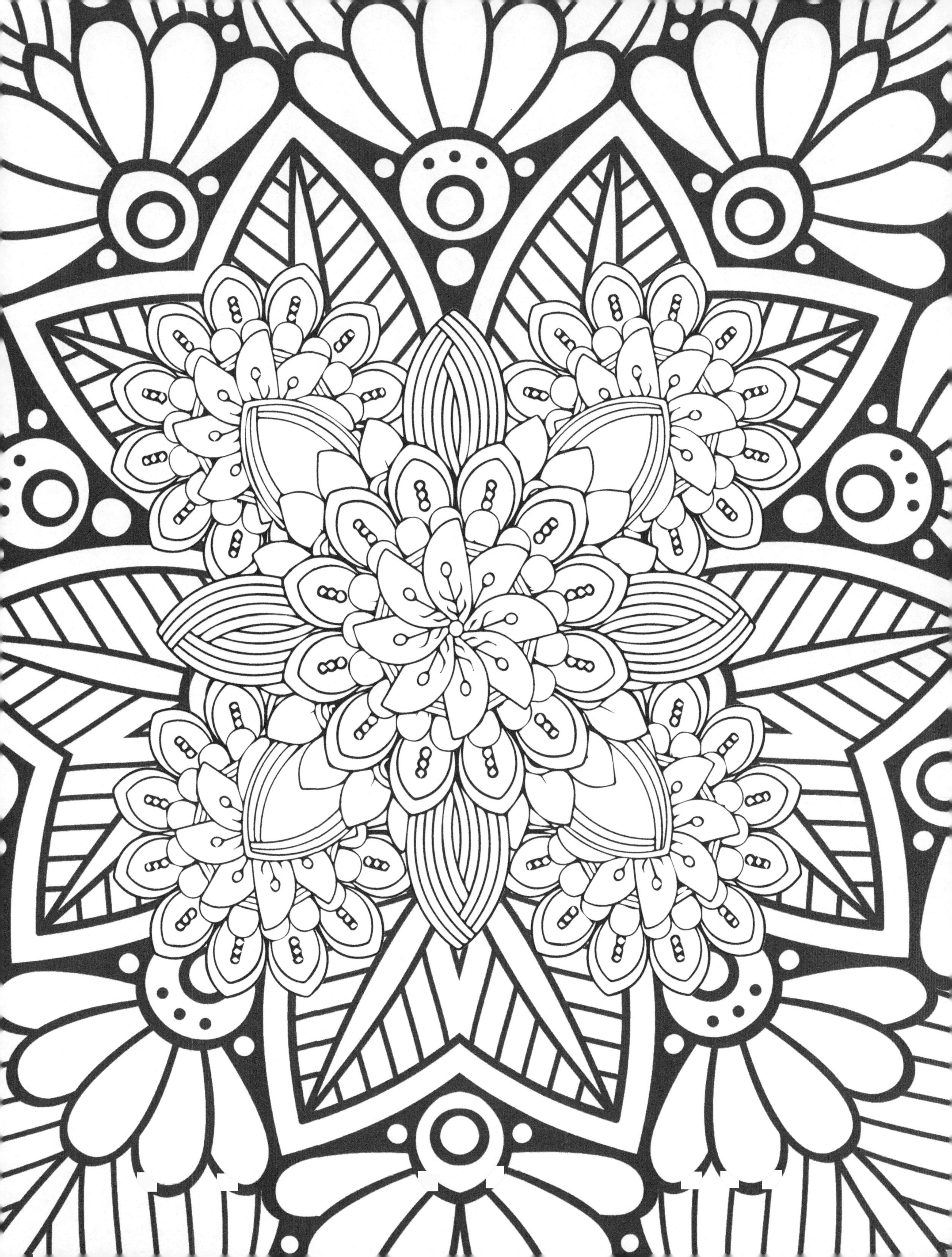

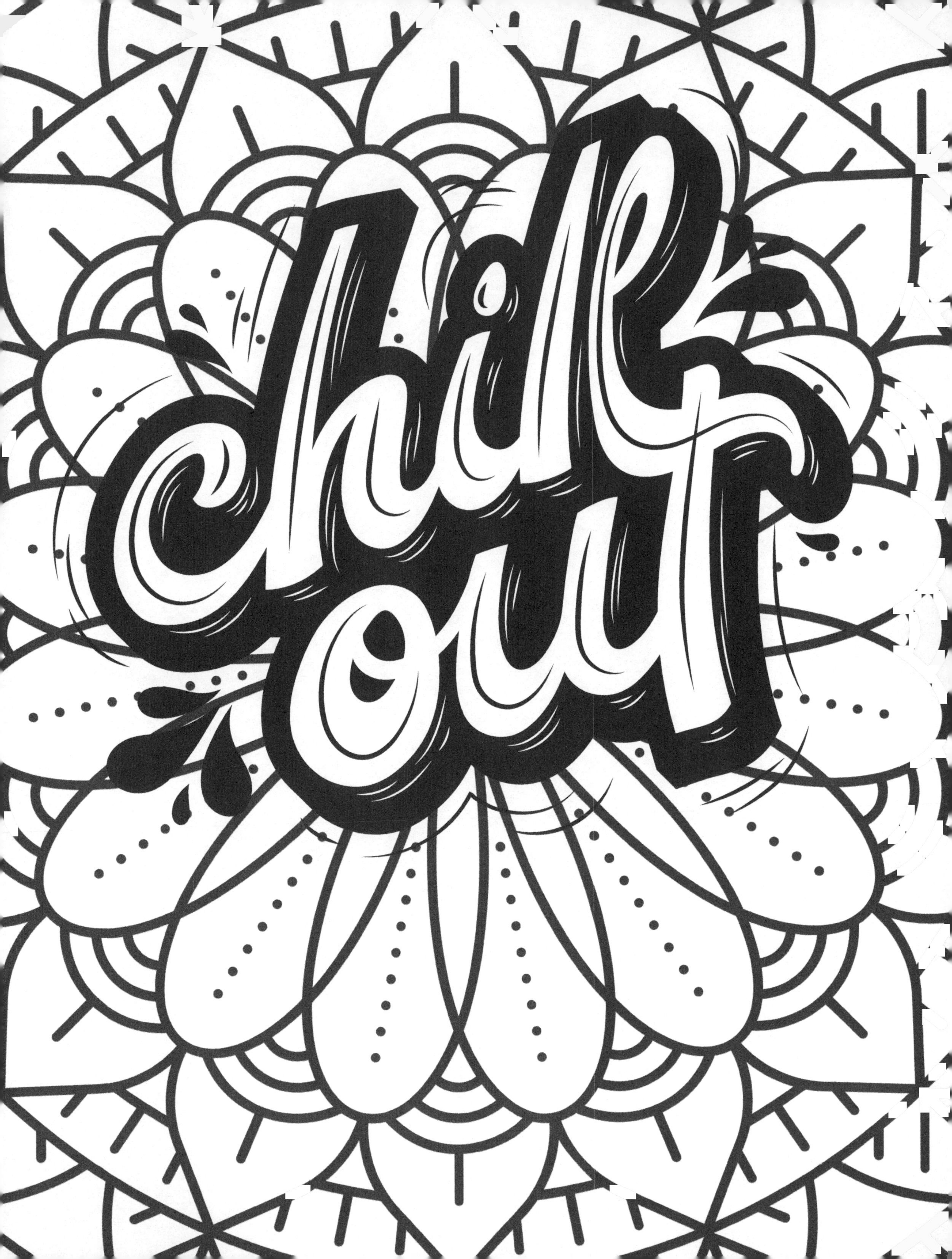
chill out

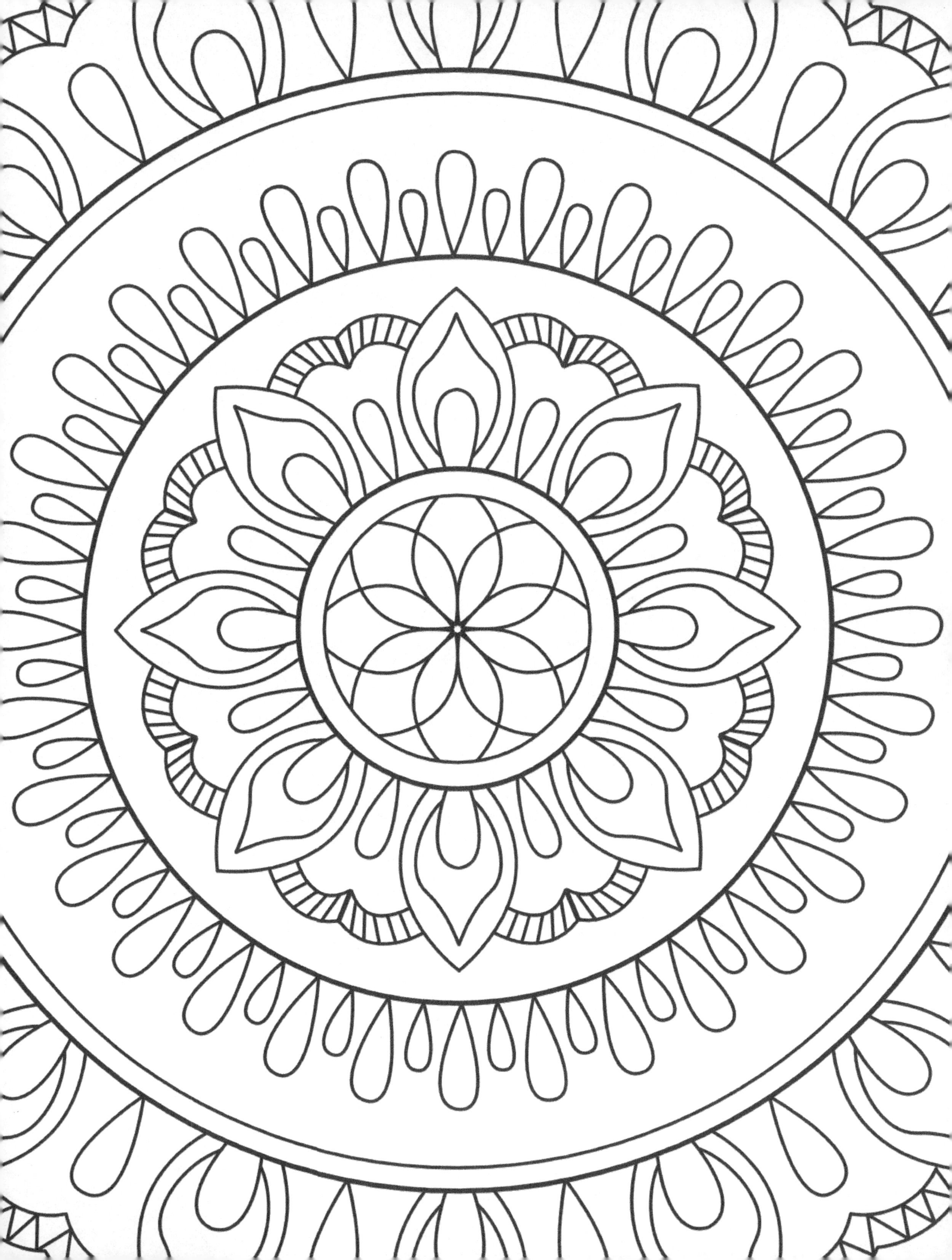

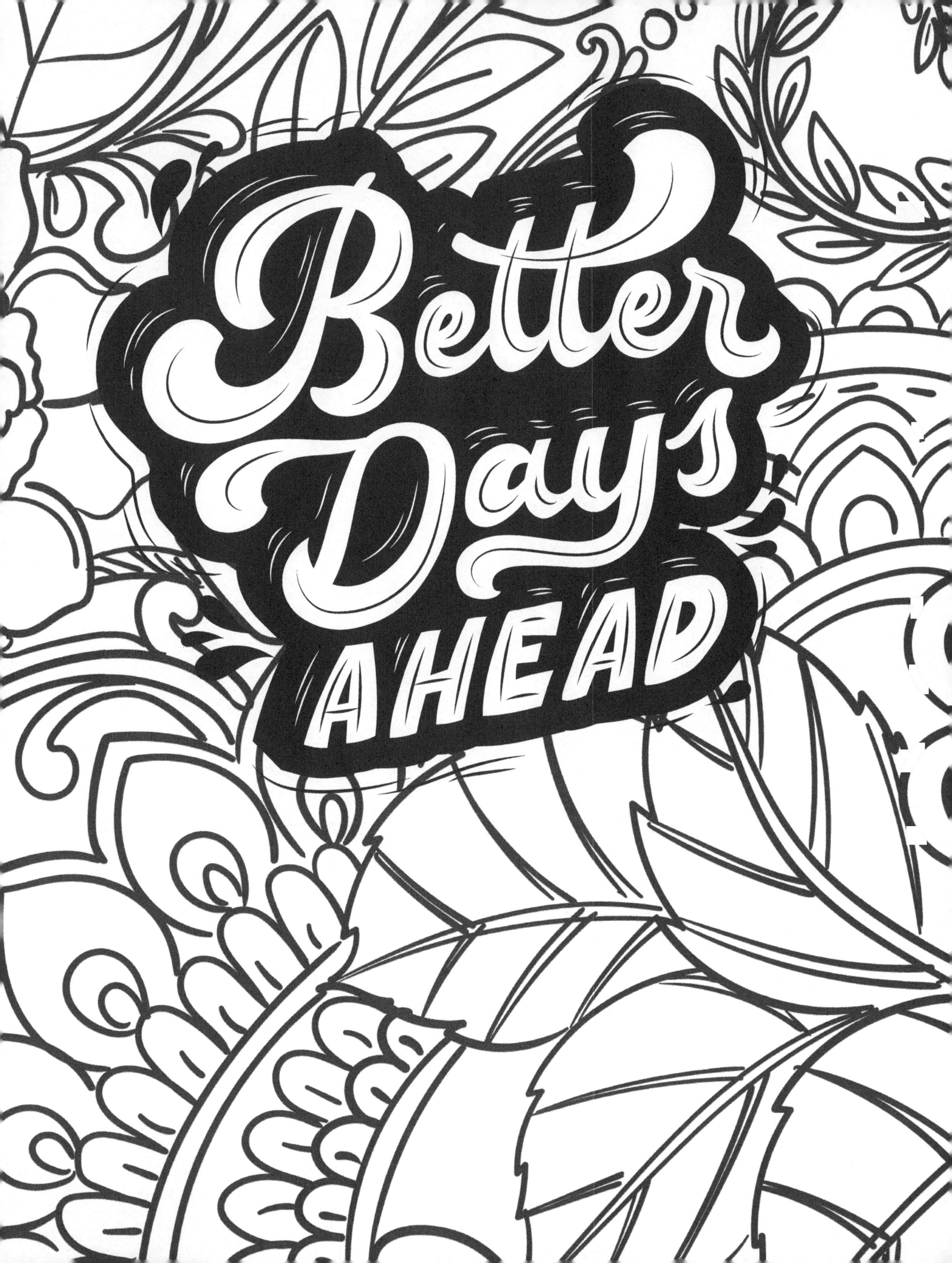
Better Days
AHEAD

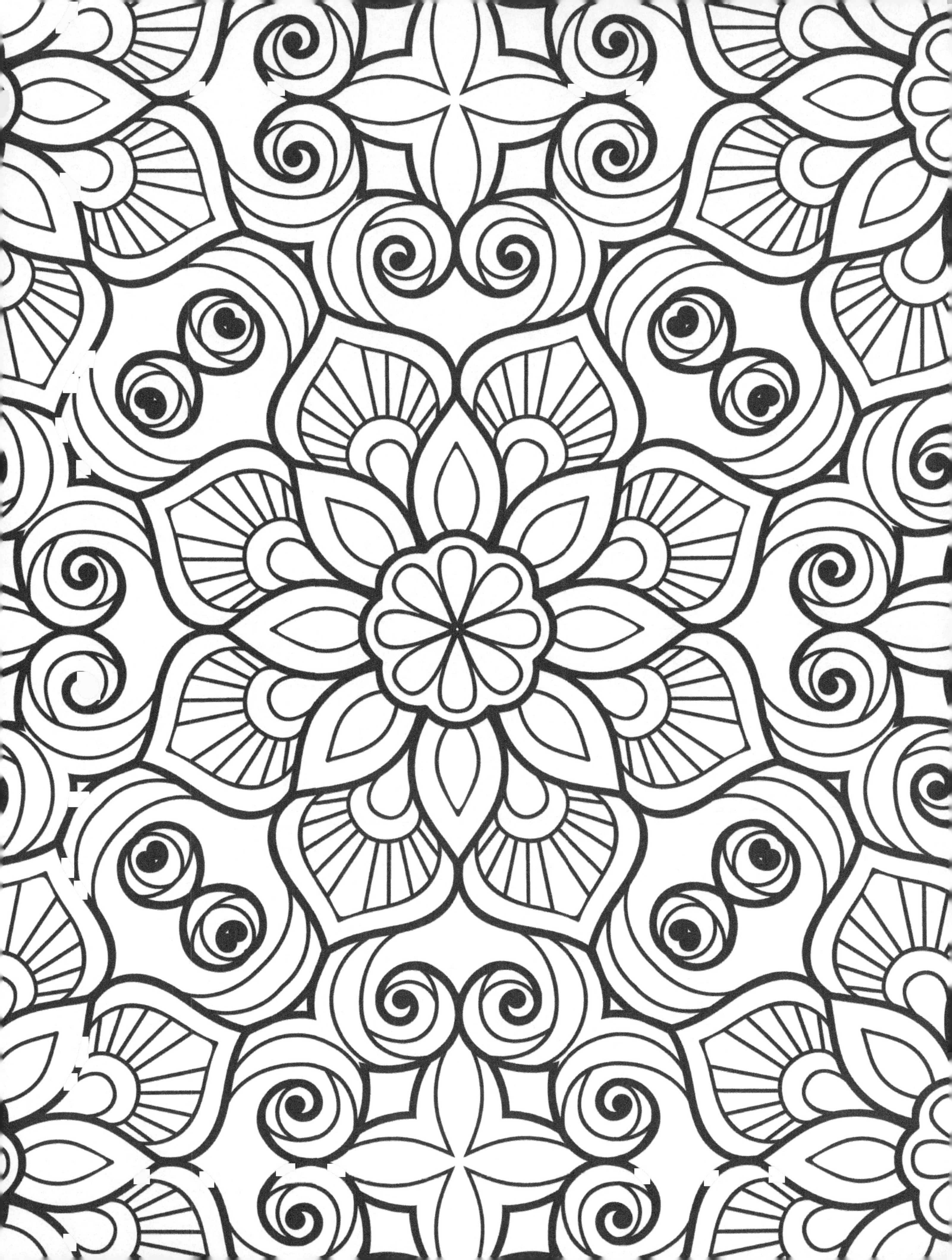

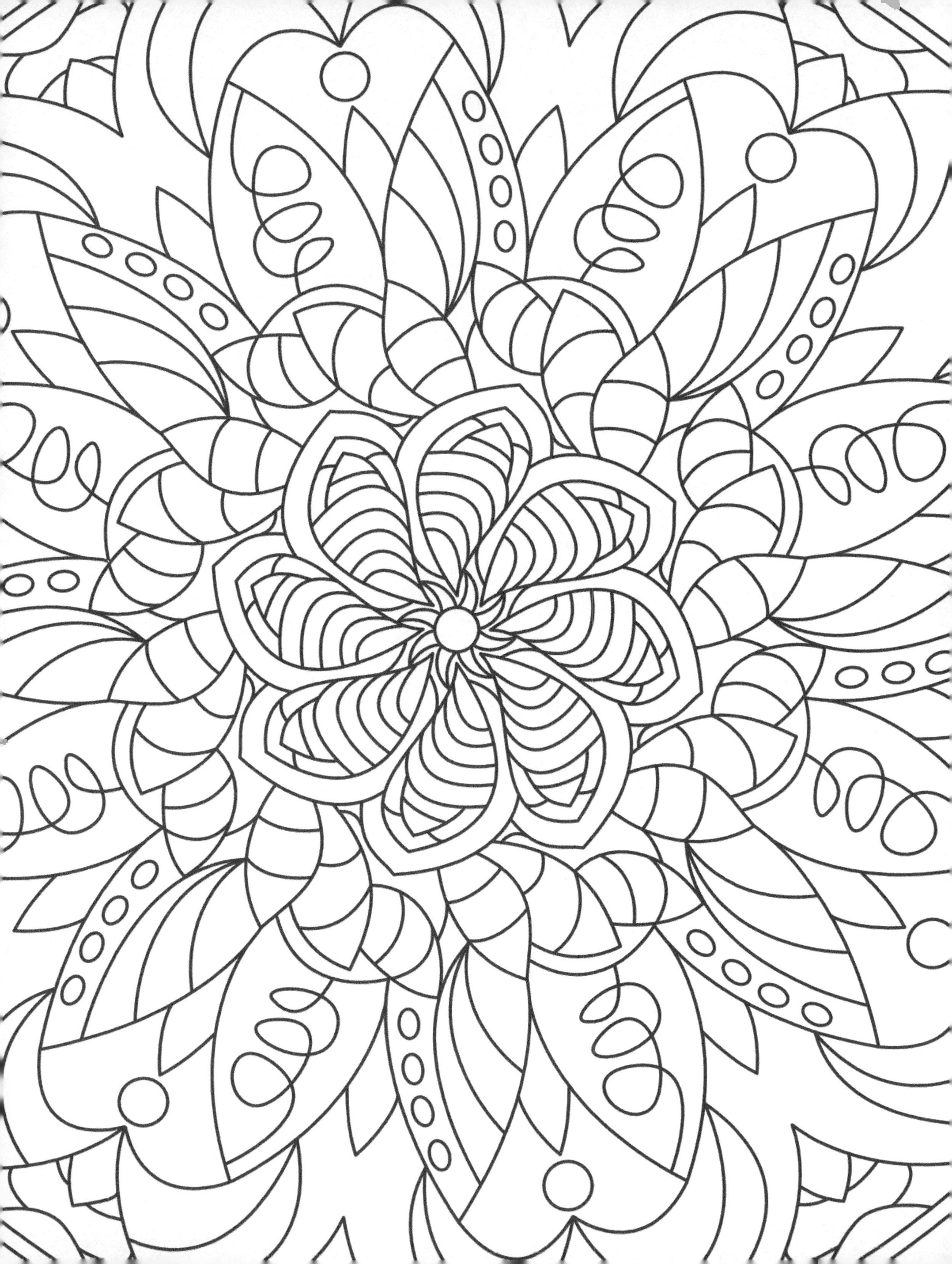

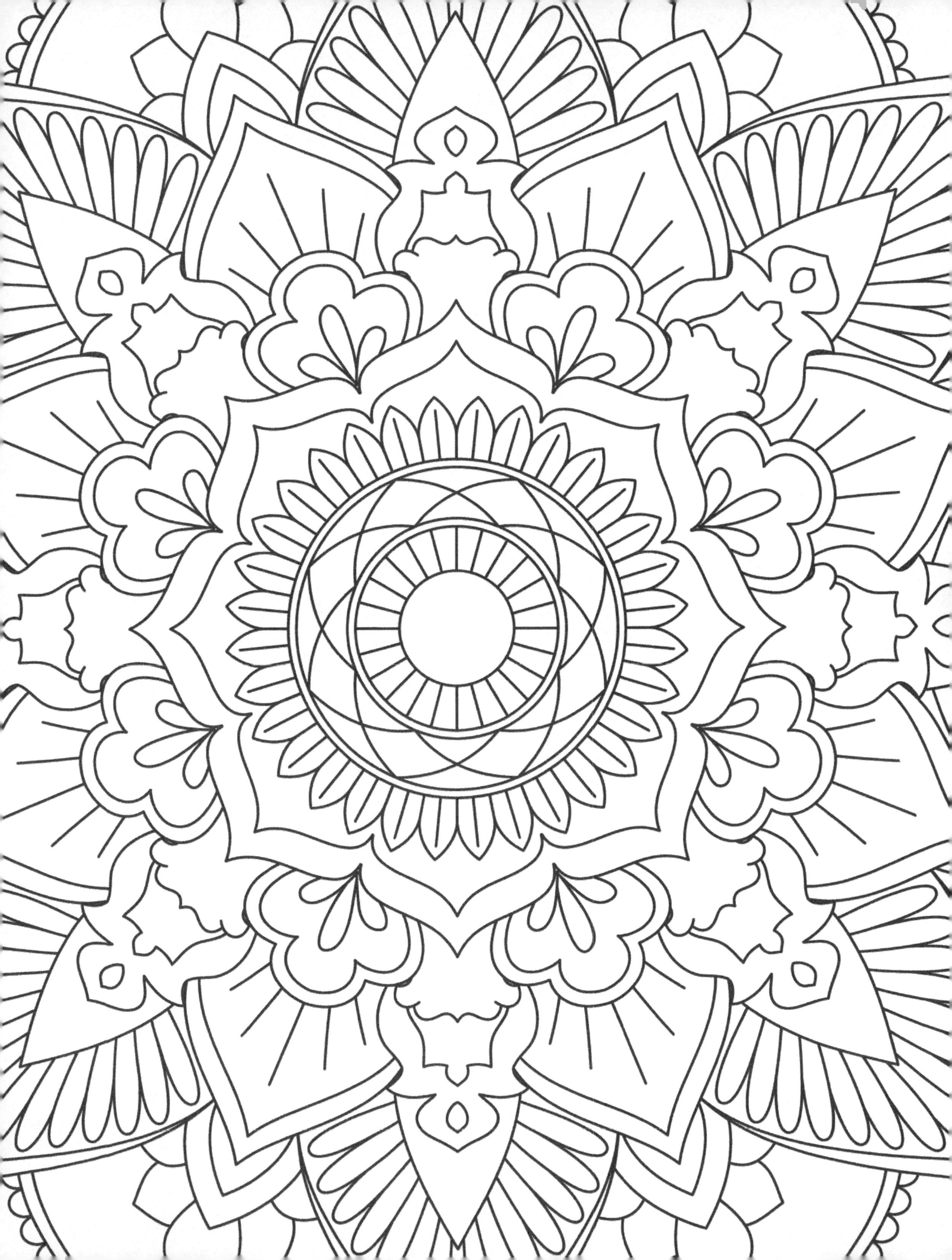

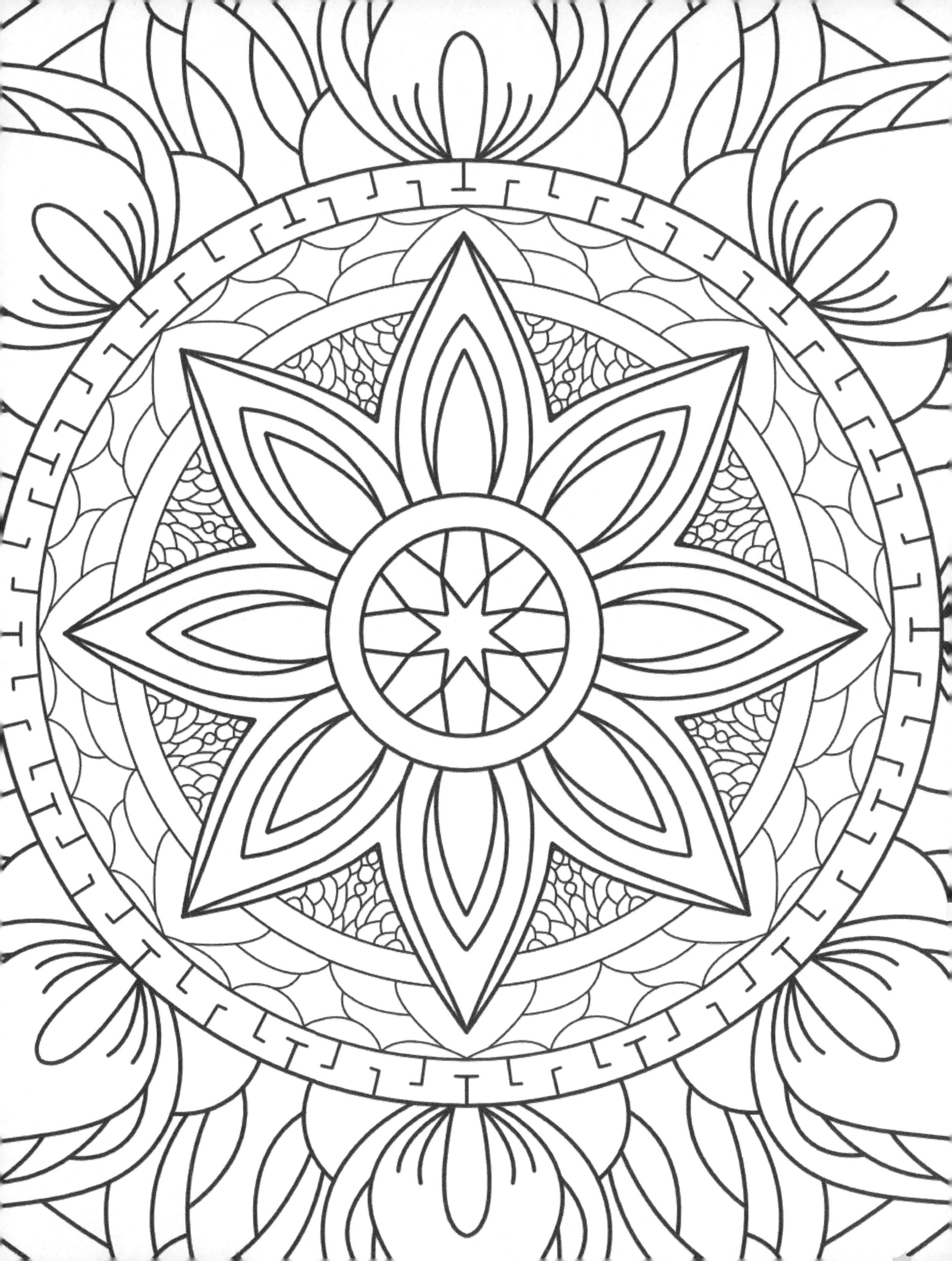

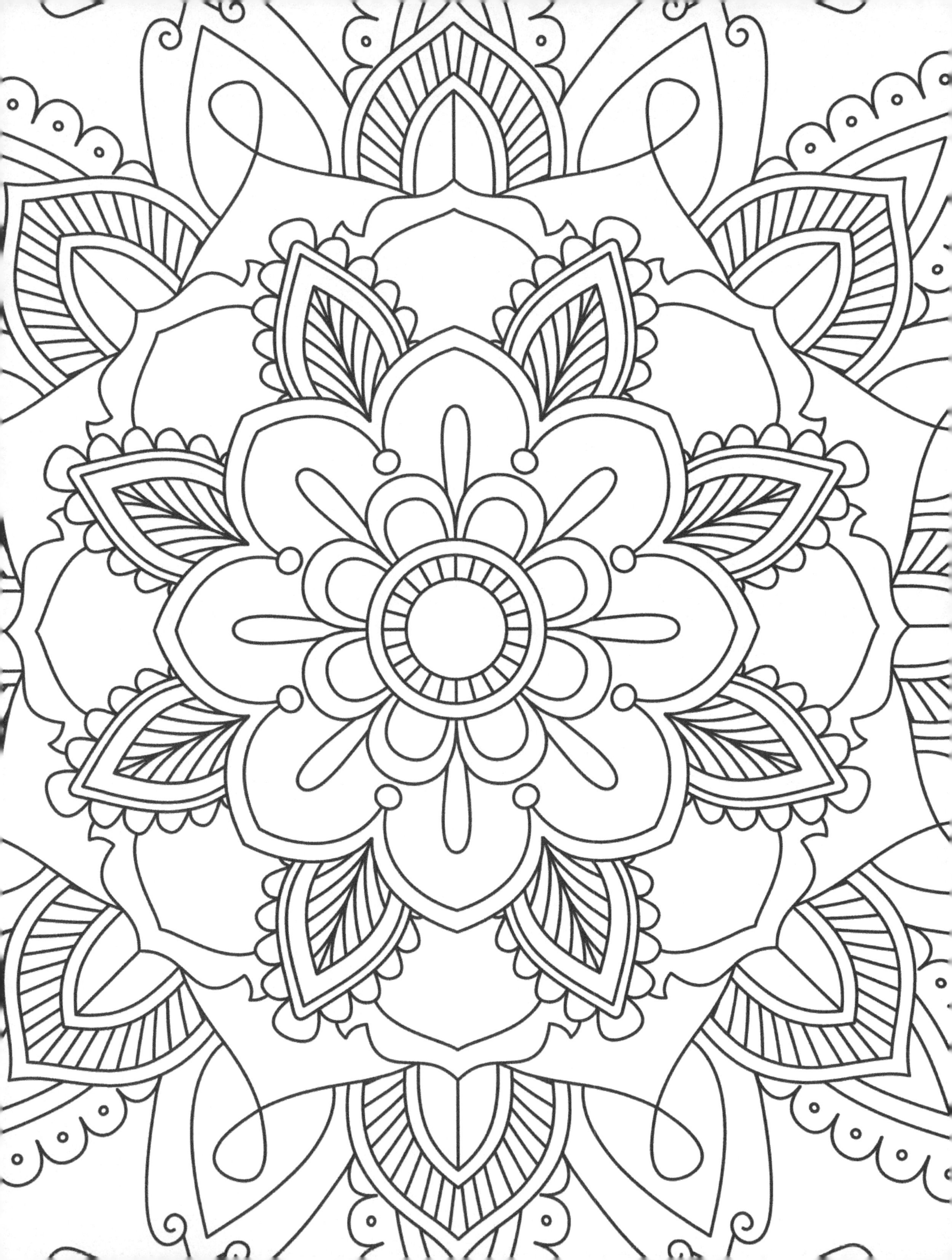

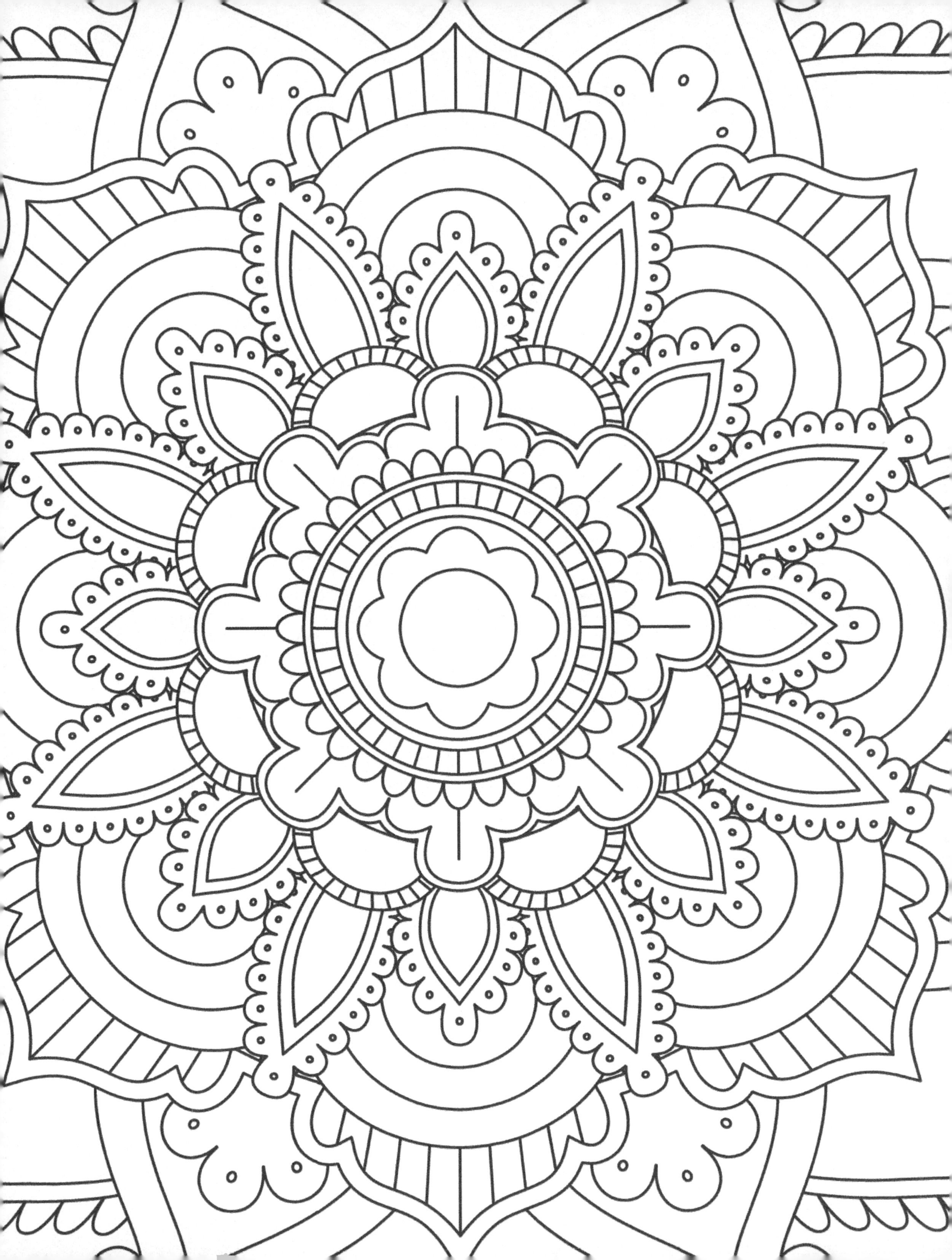

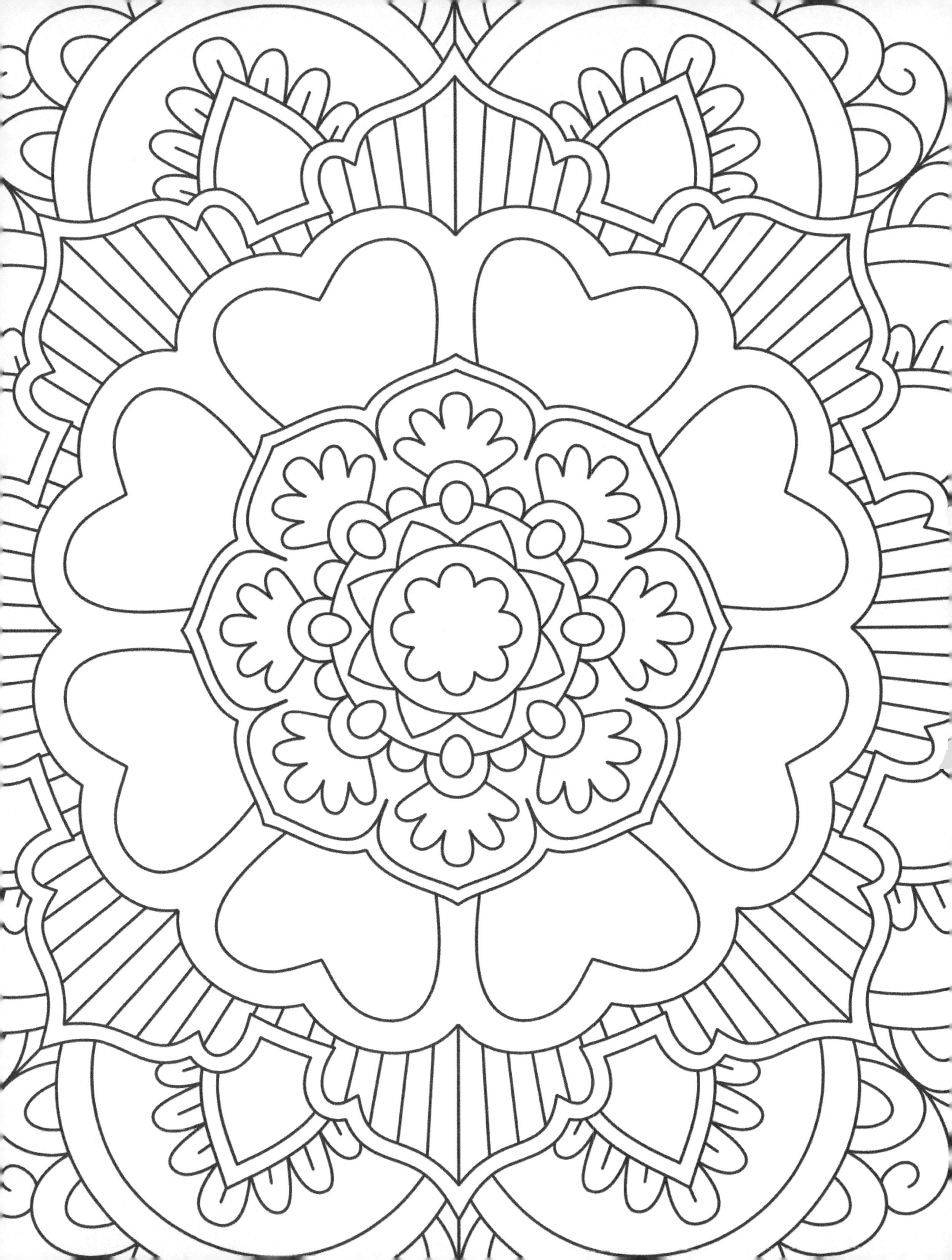

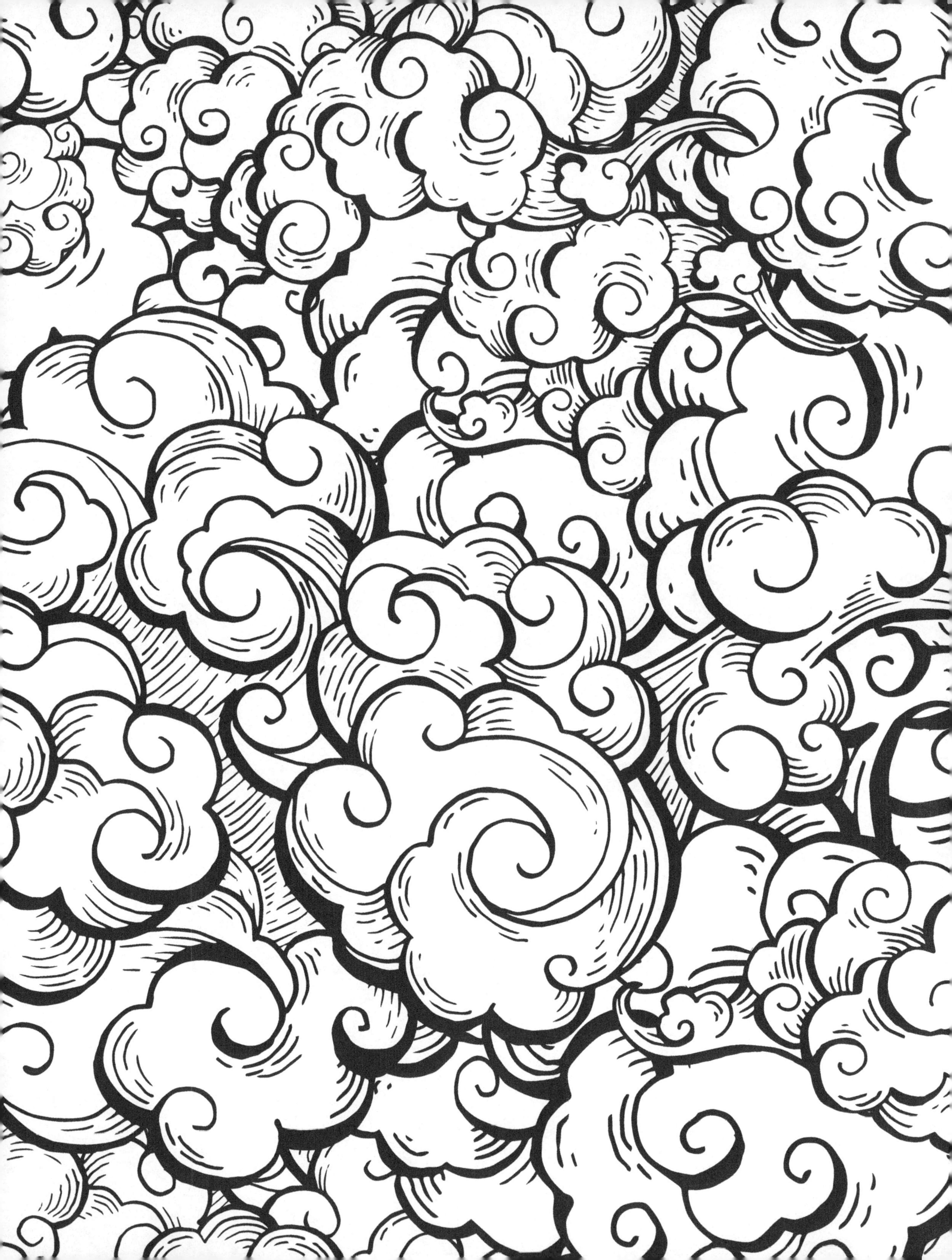

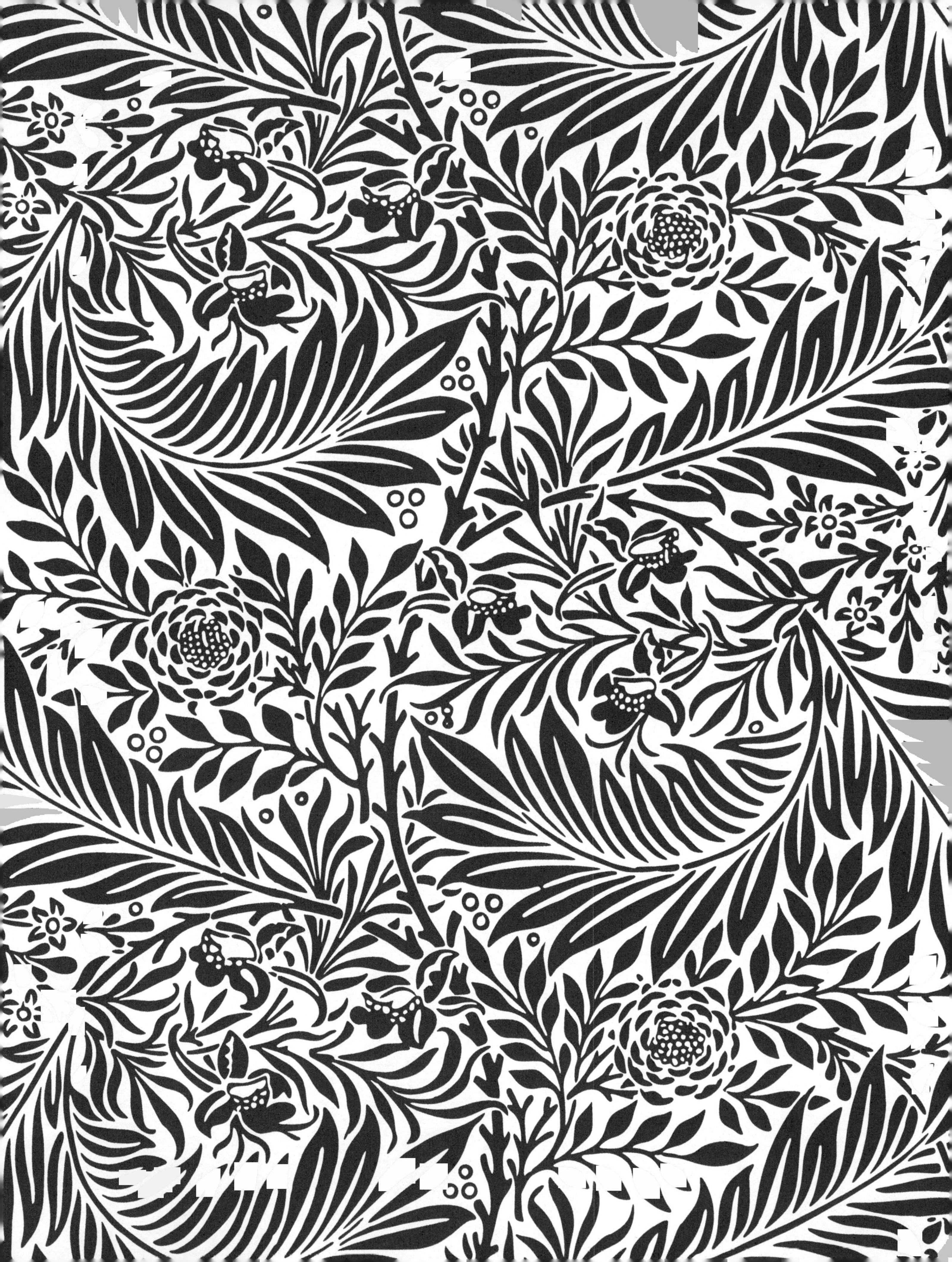

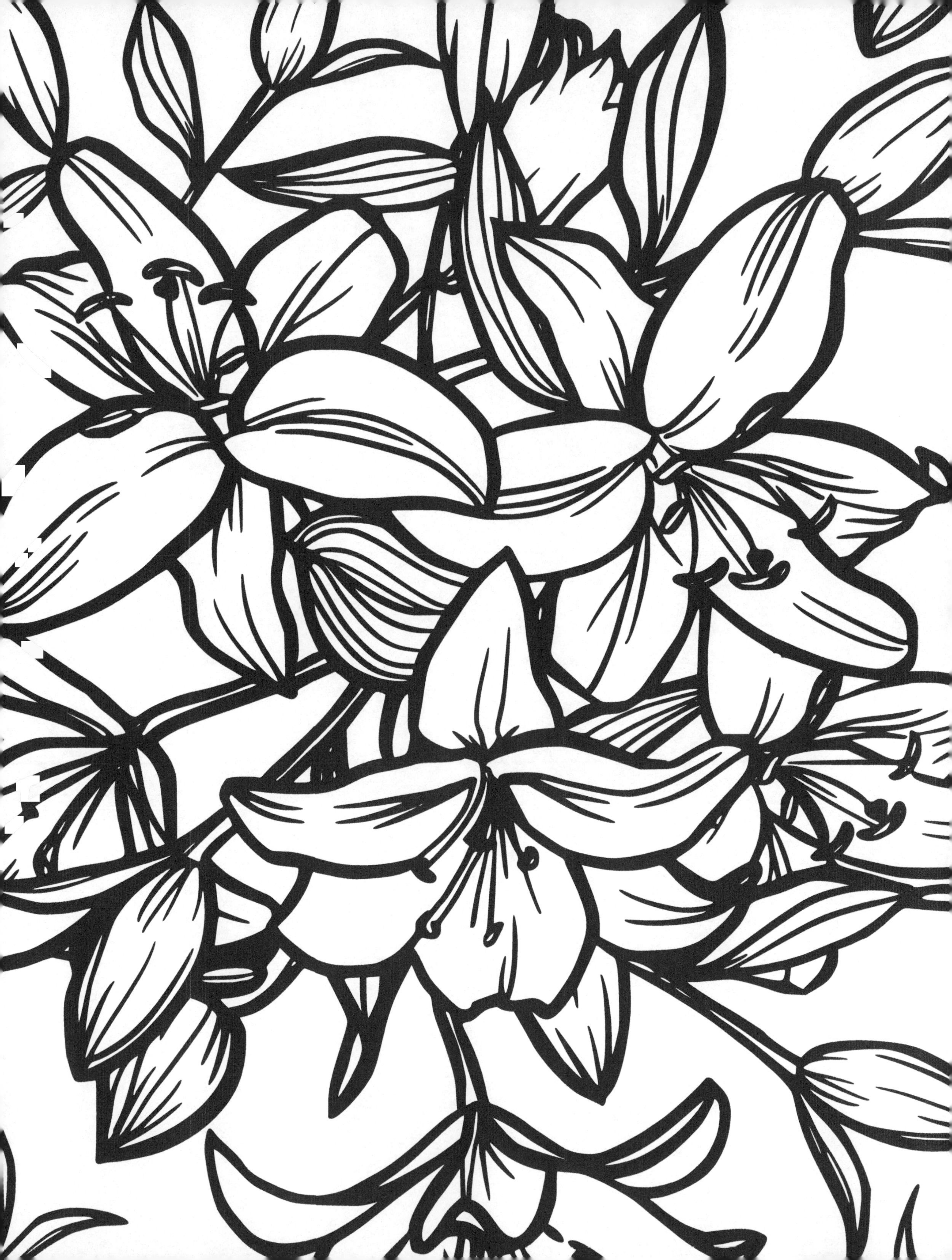

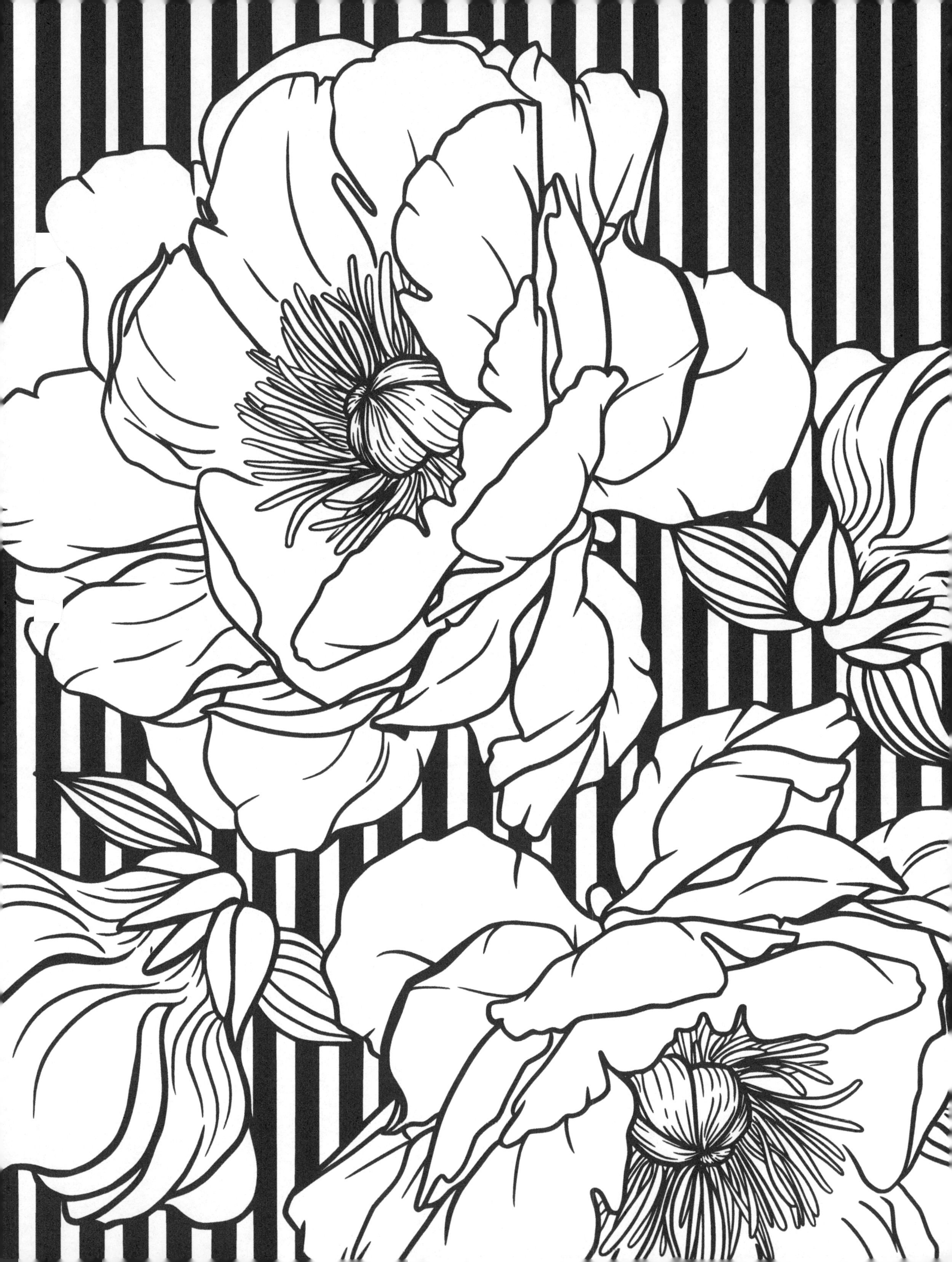

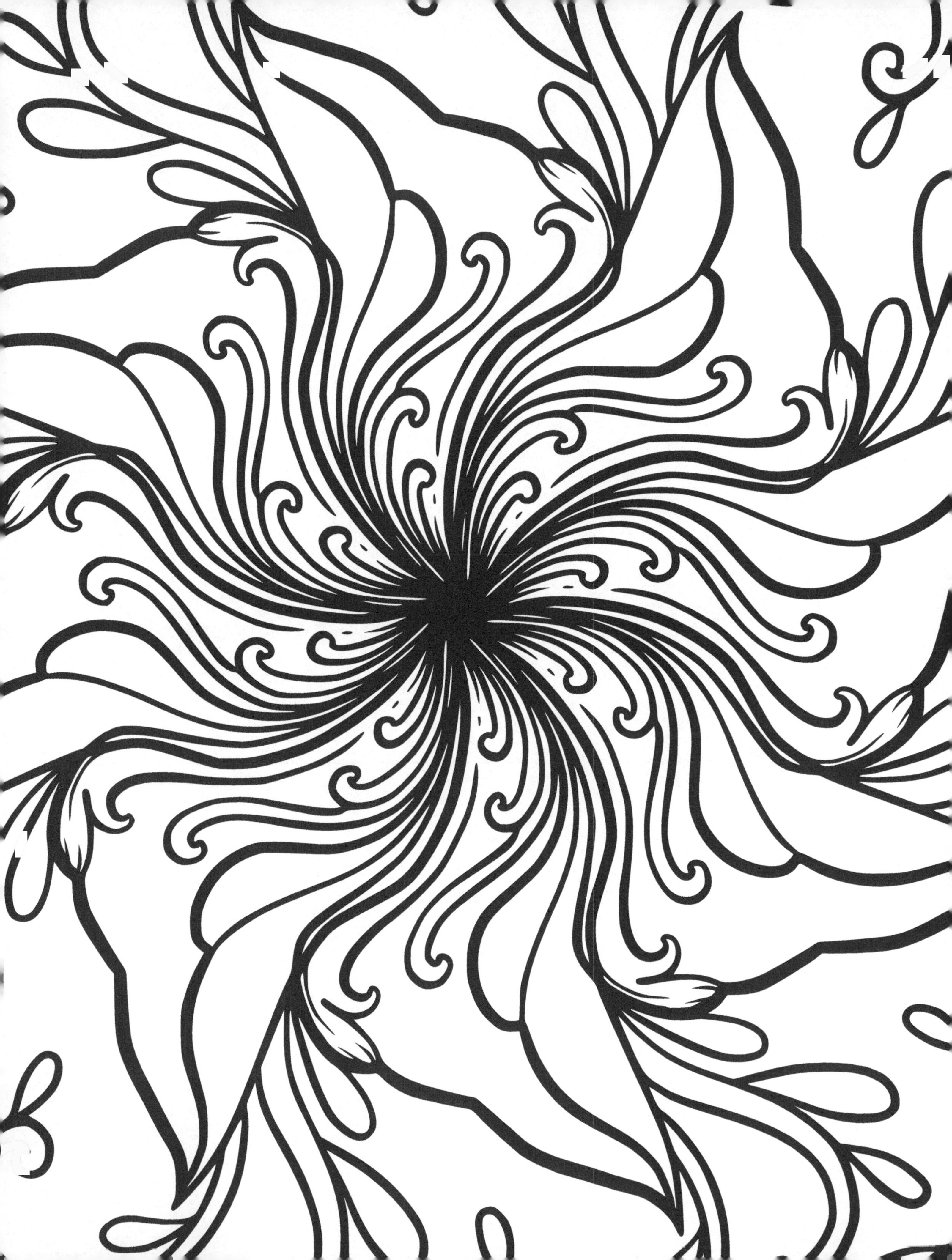

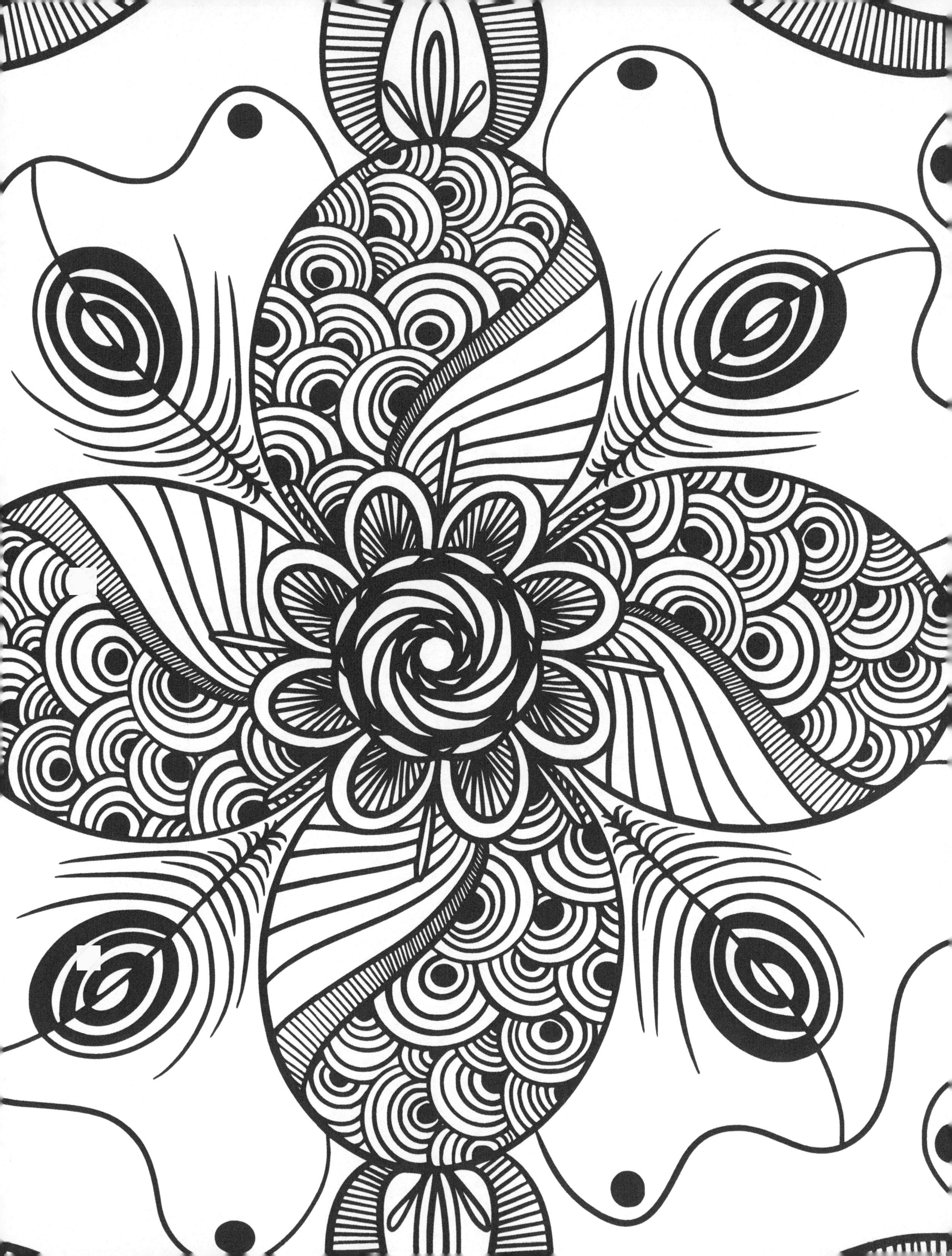

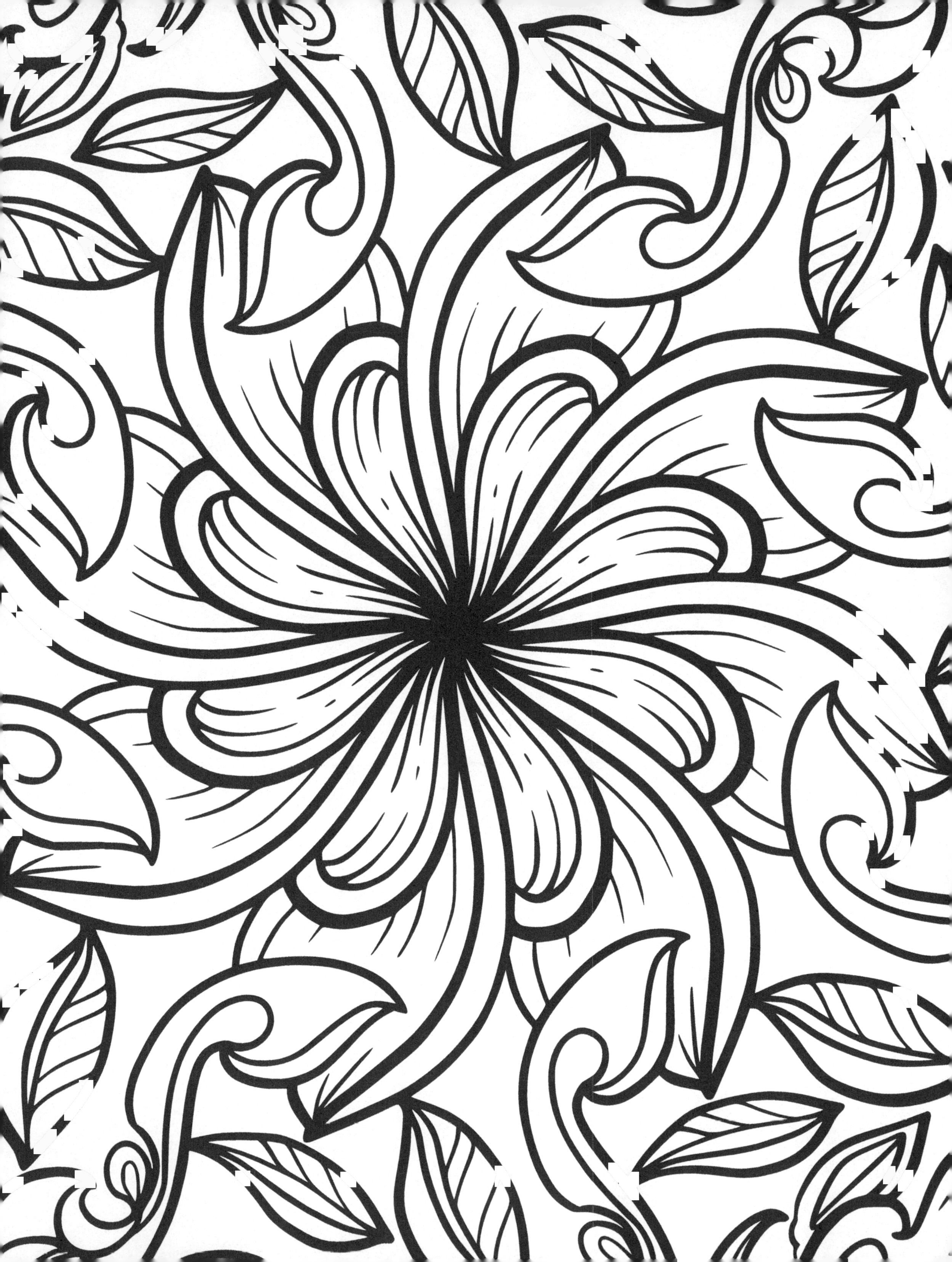

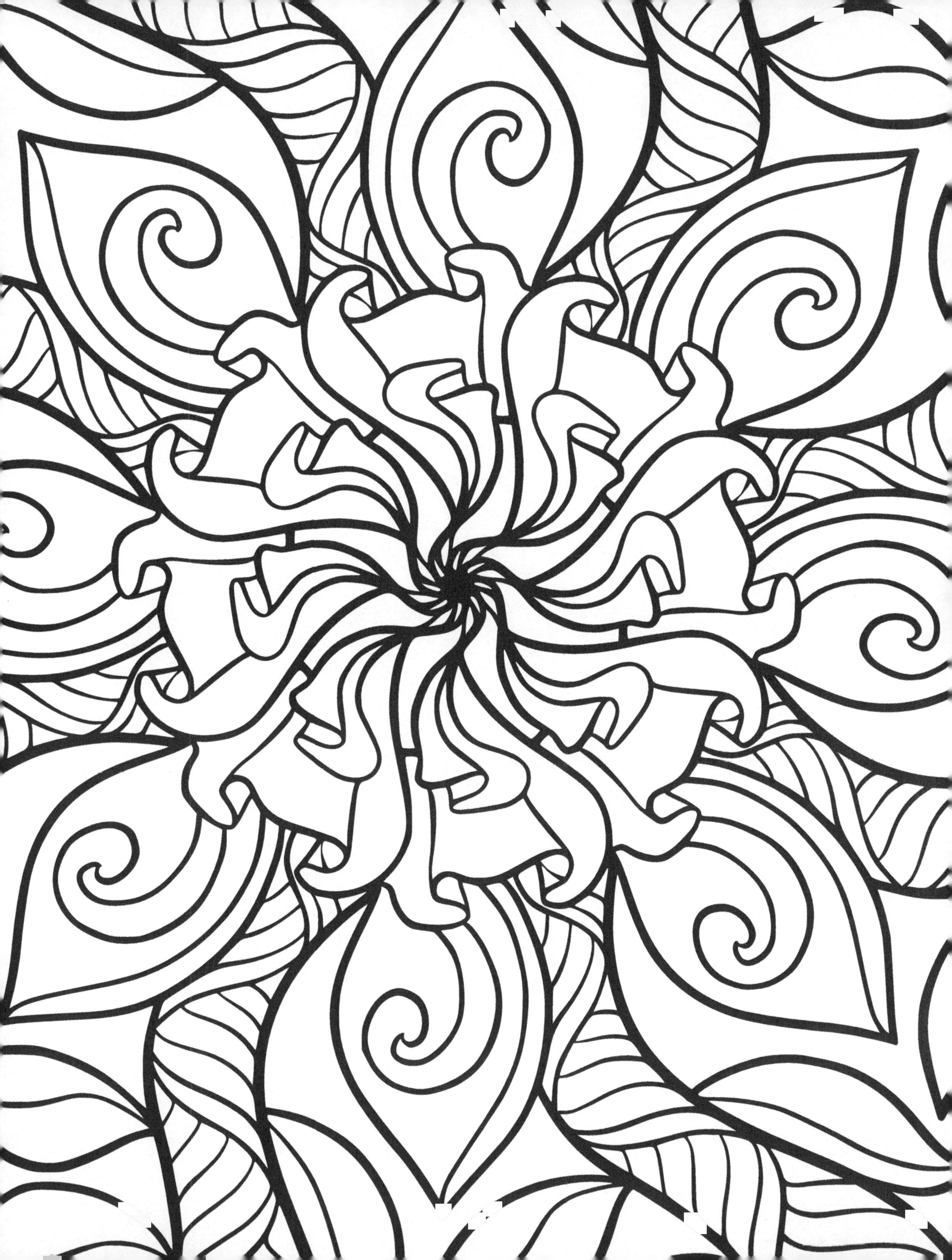

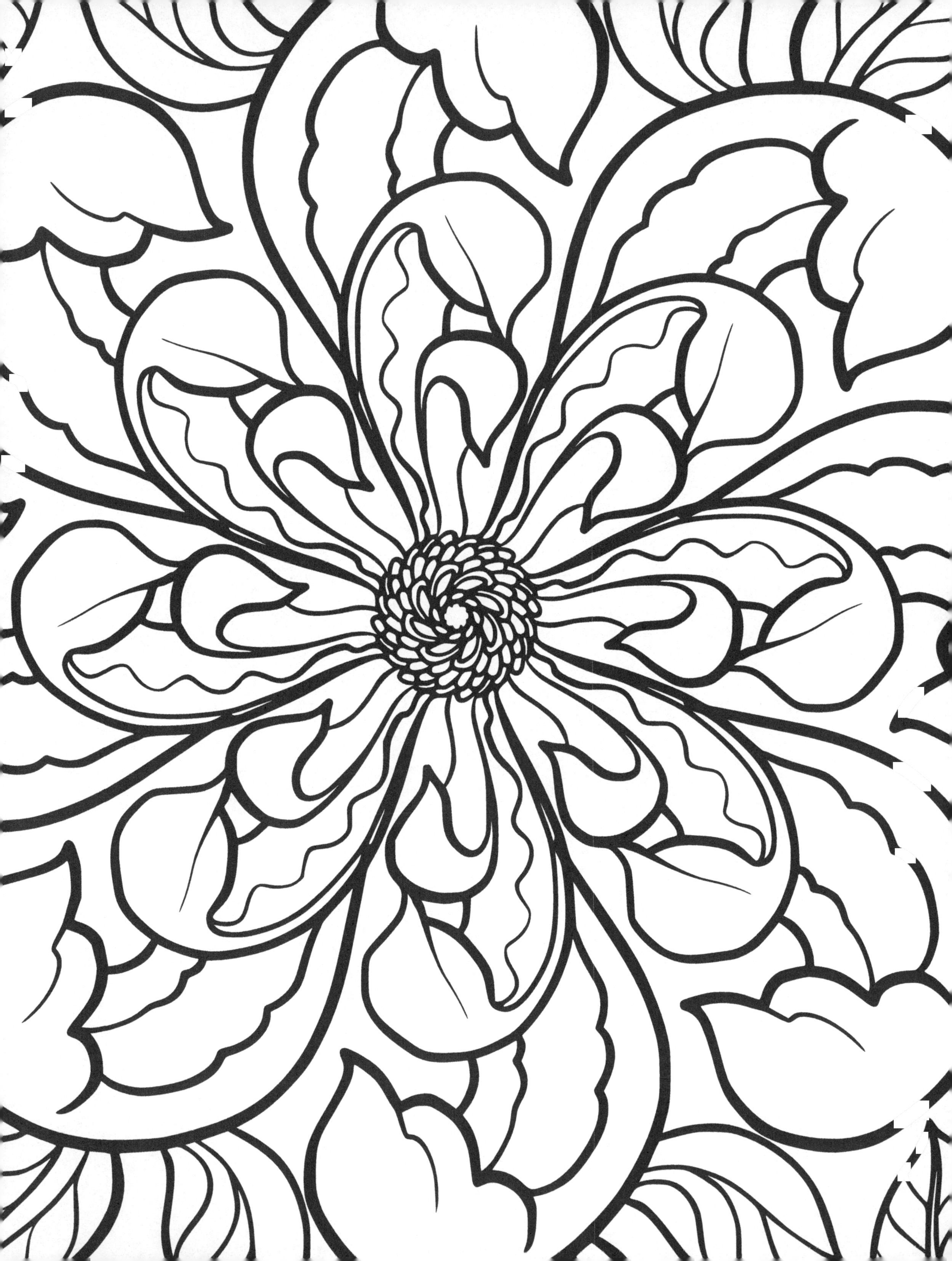

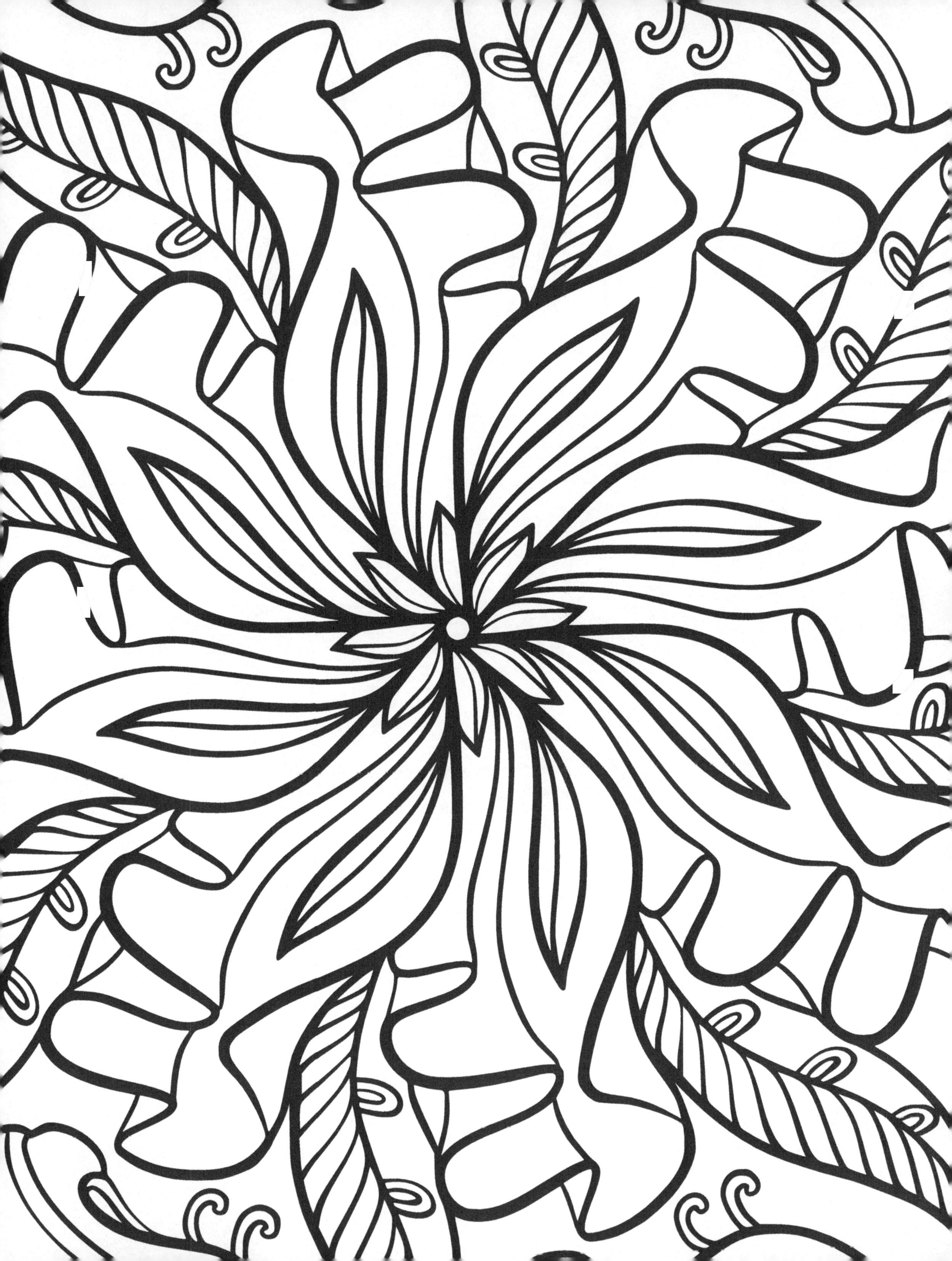

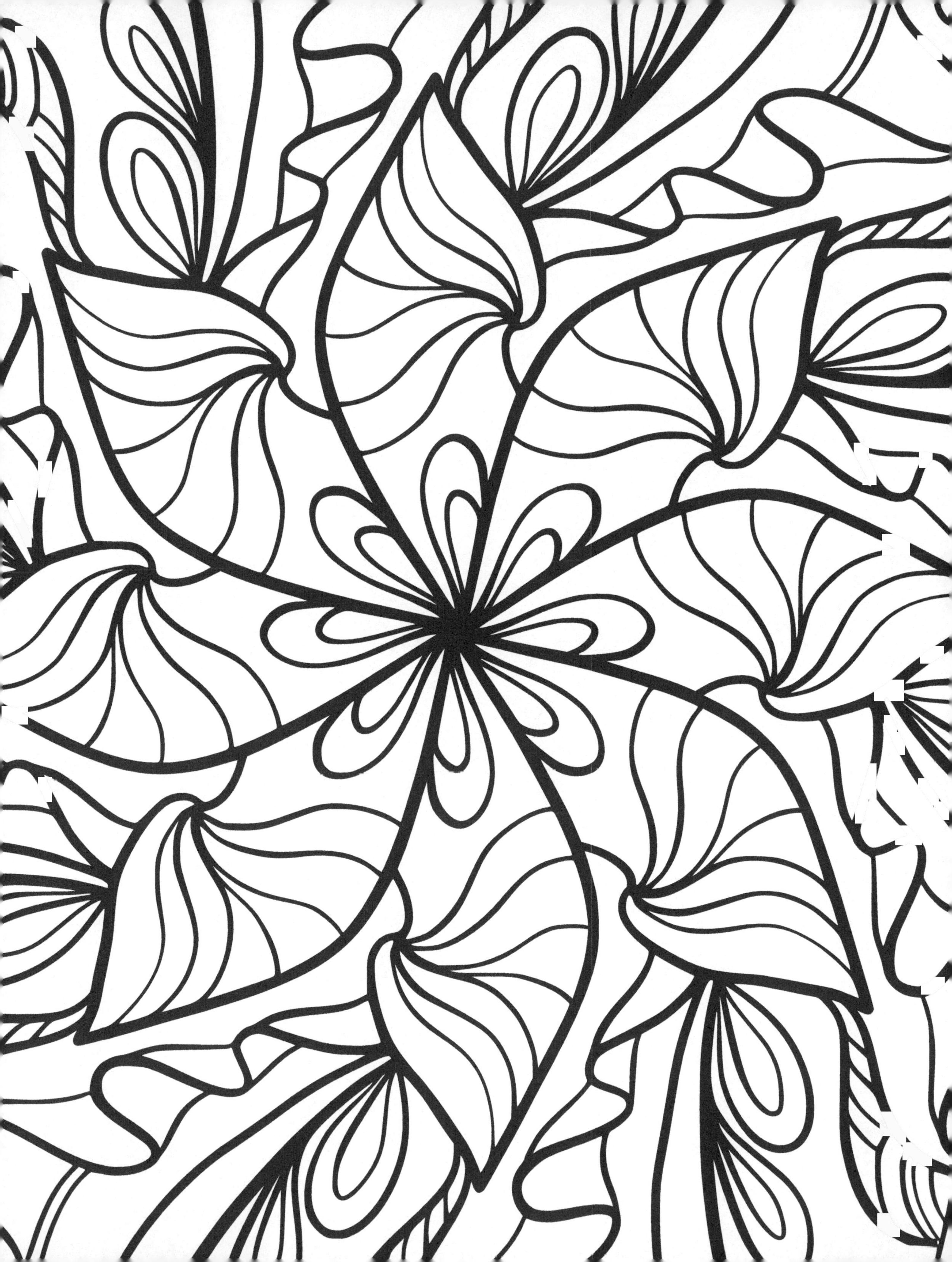

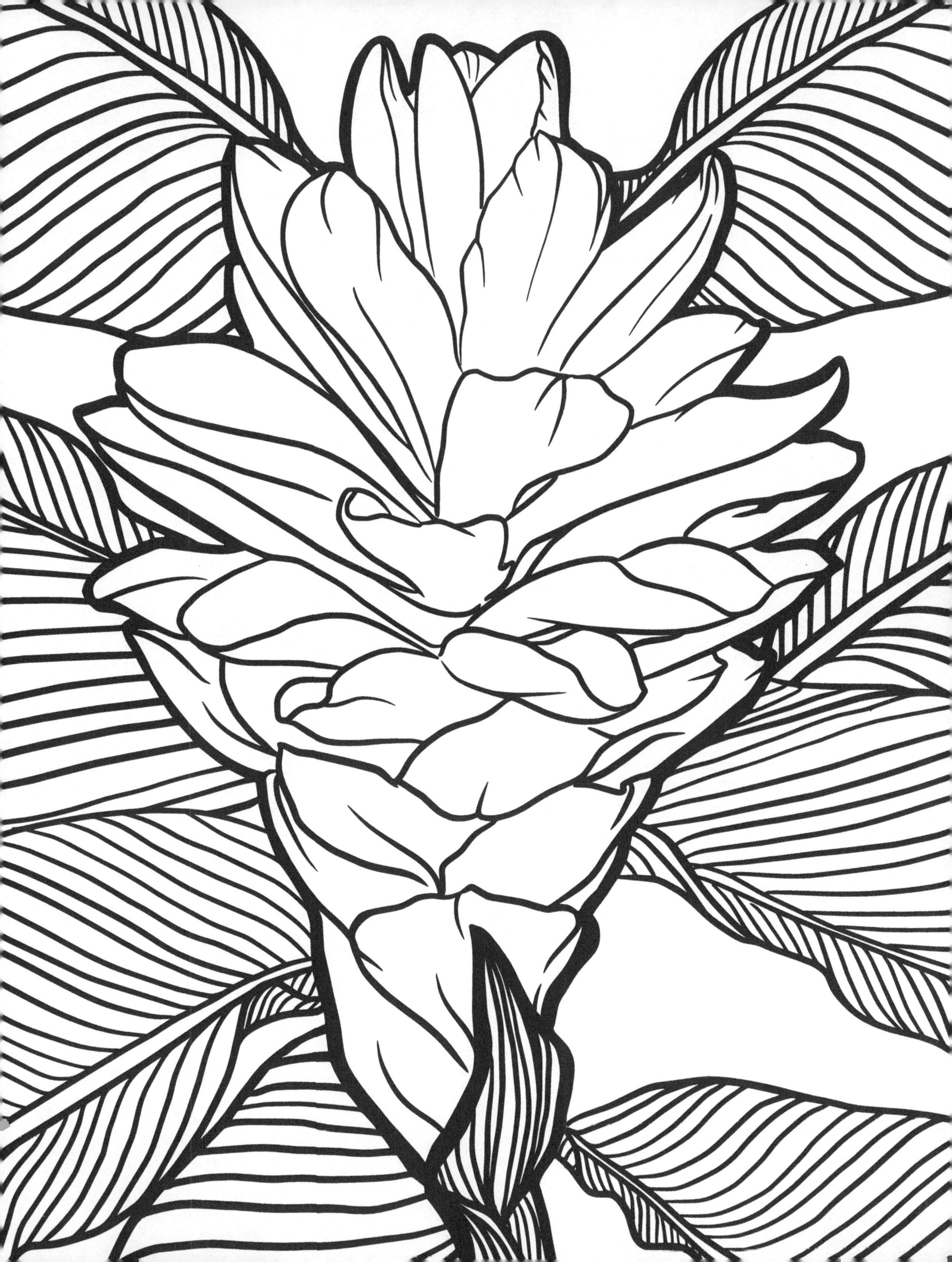

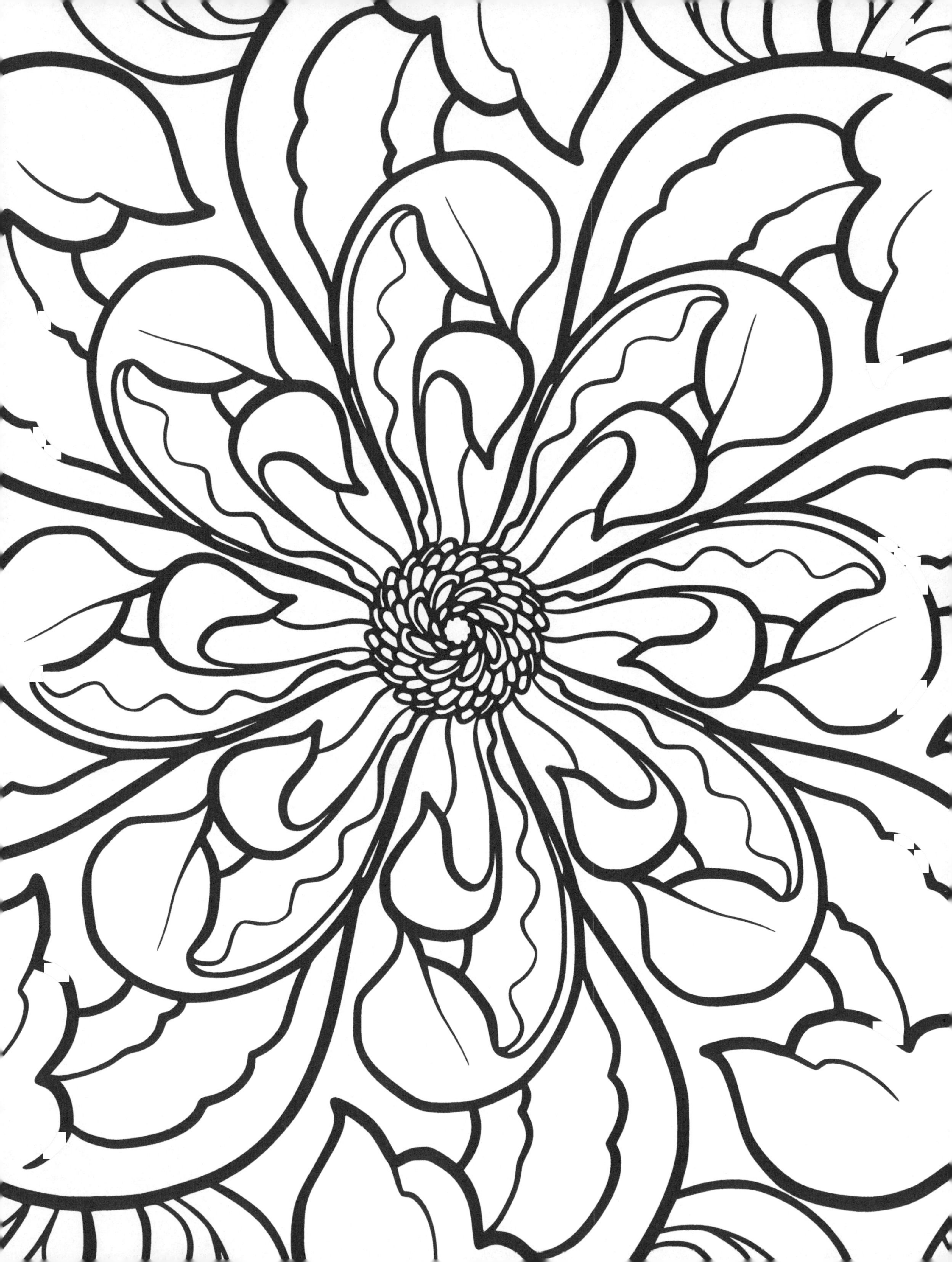

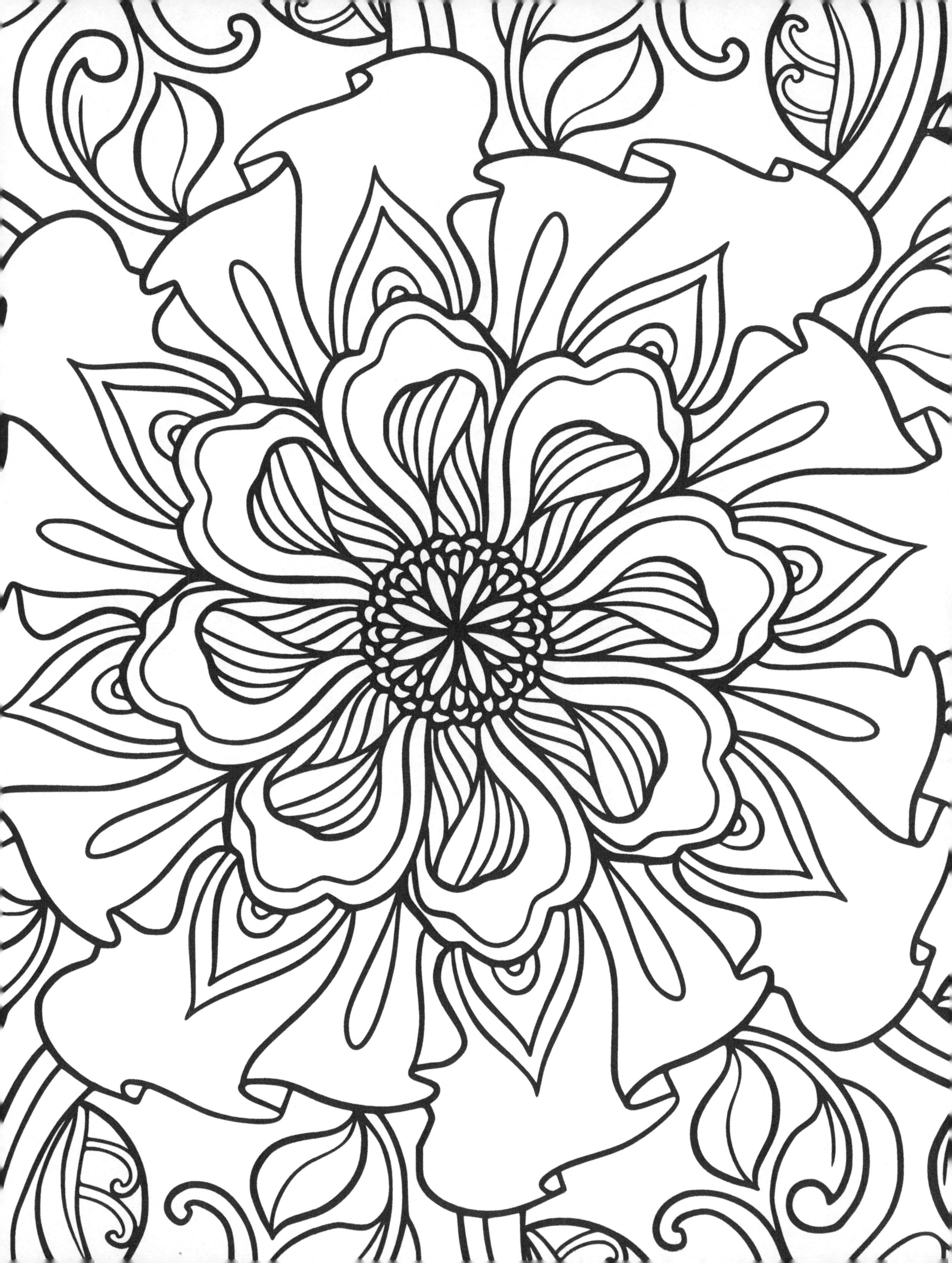

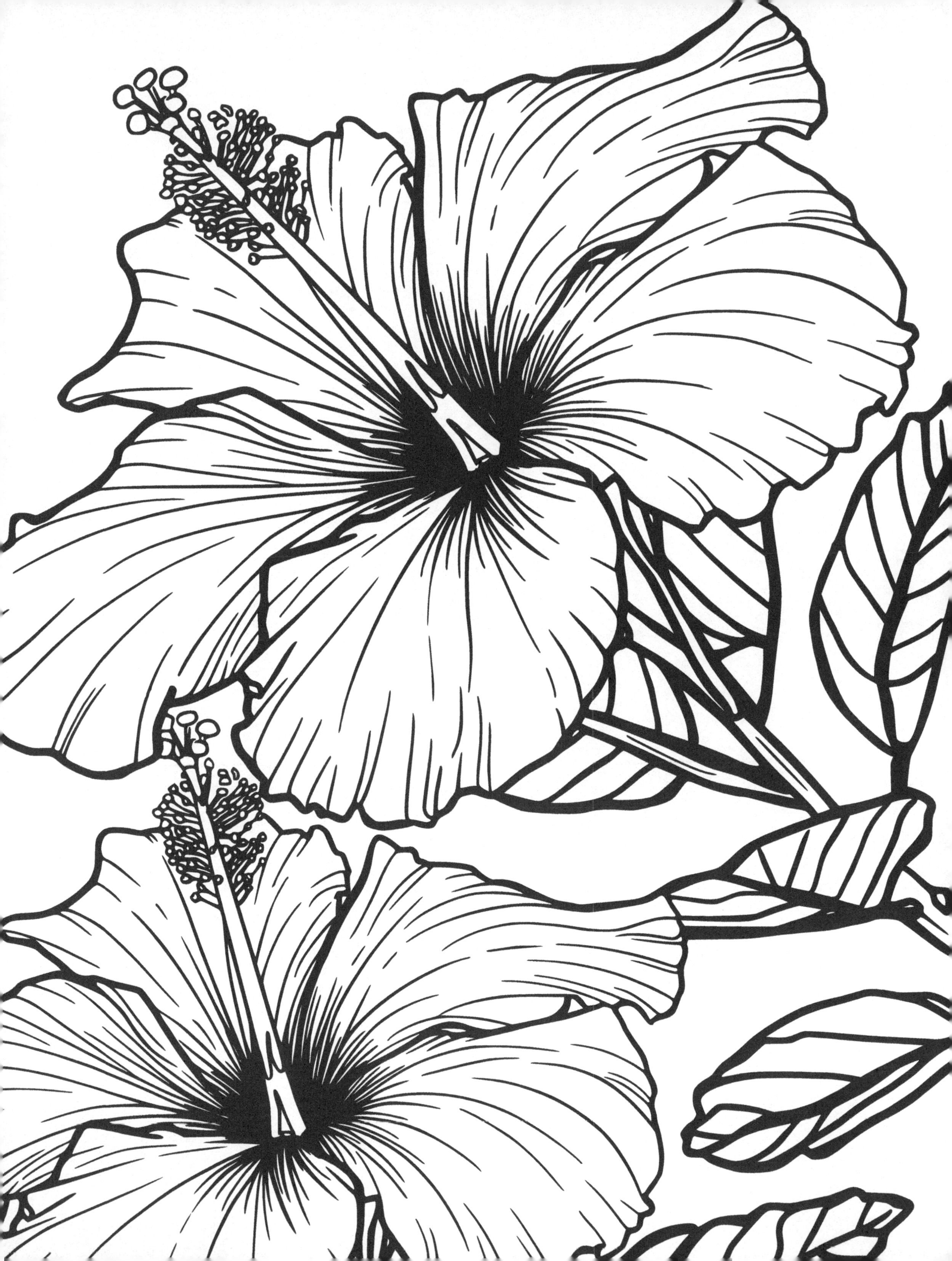

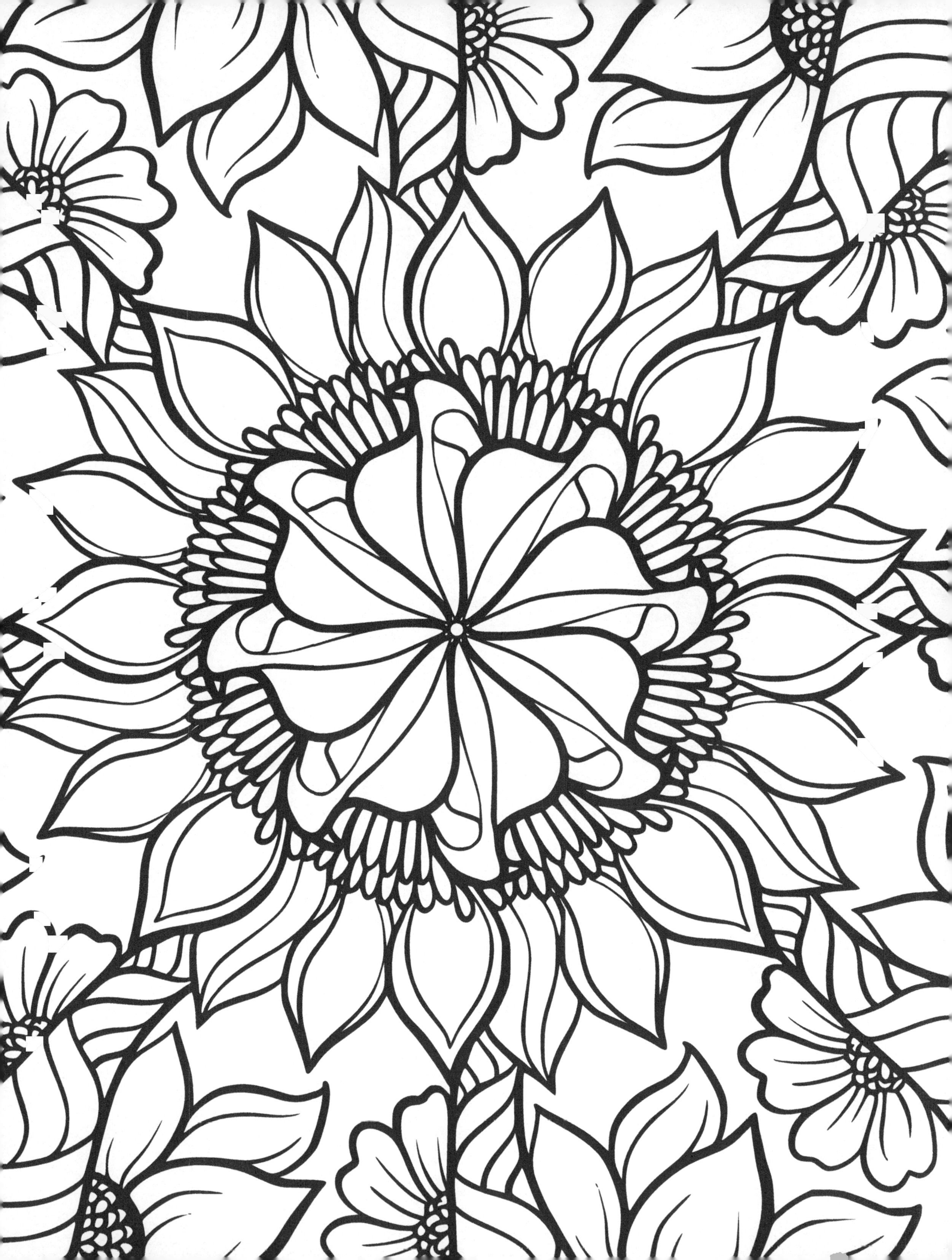

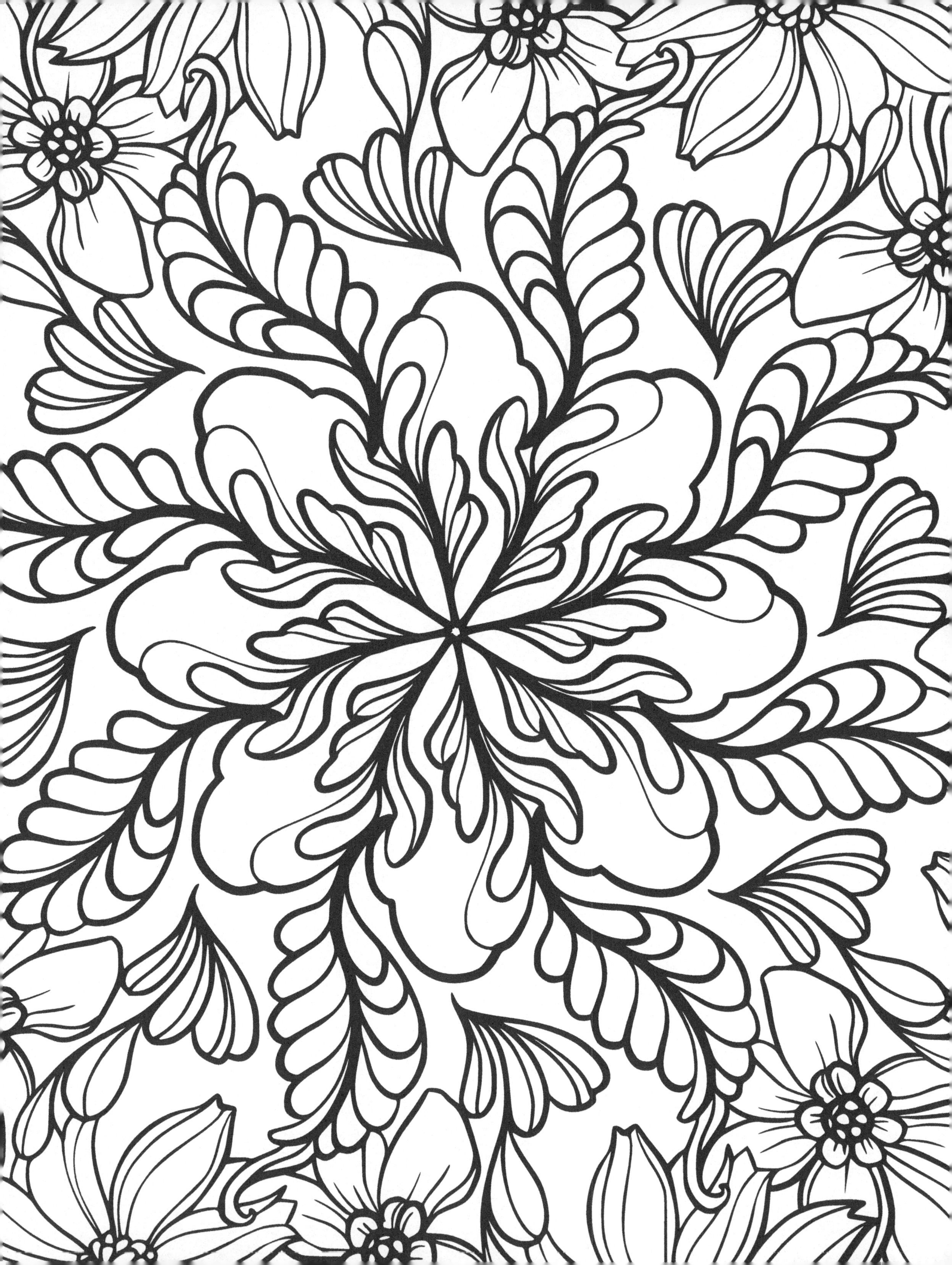

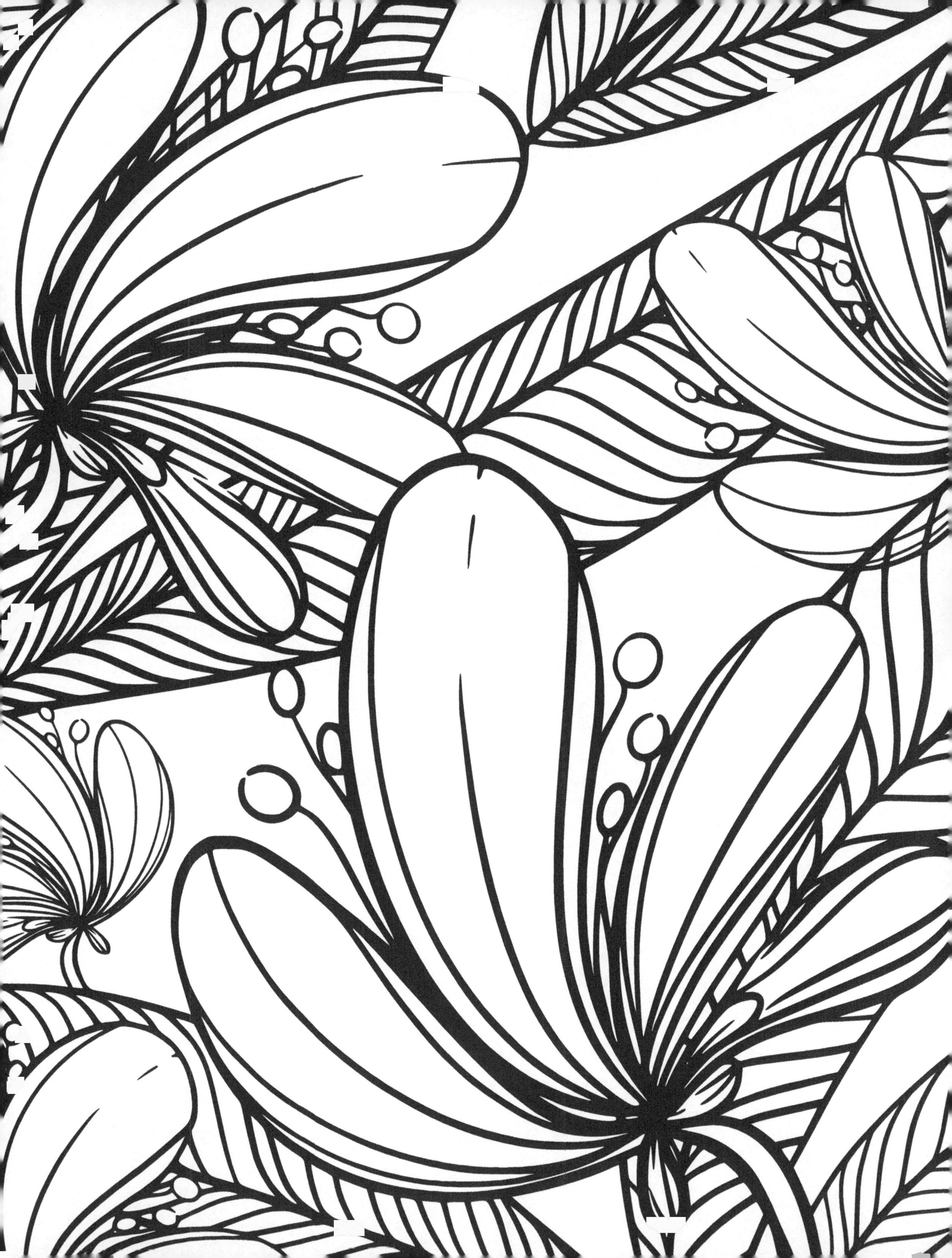

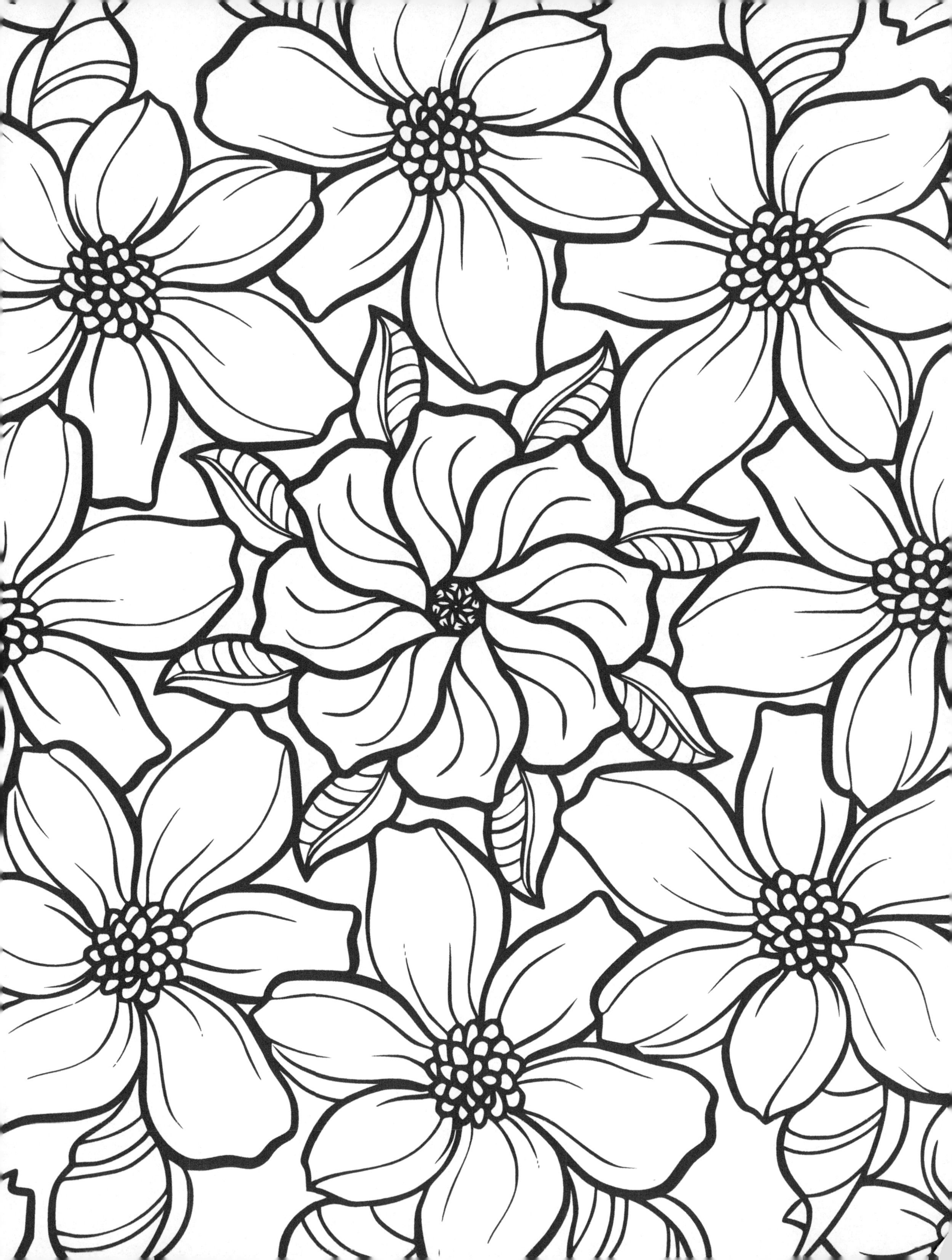

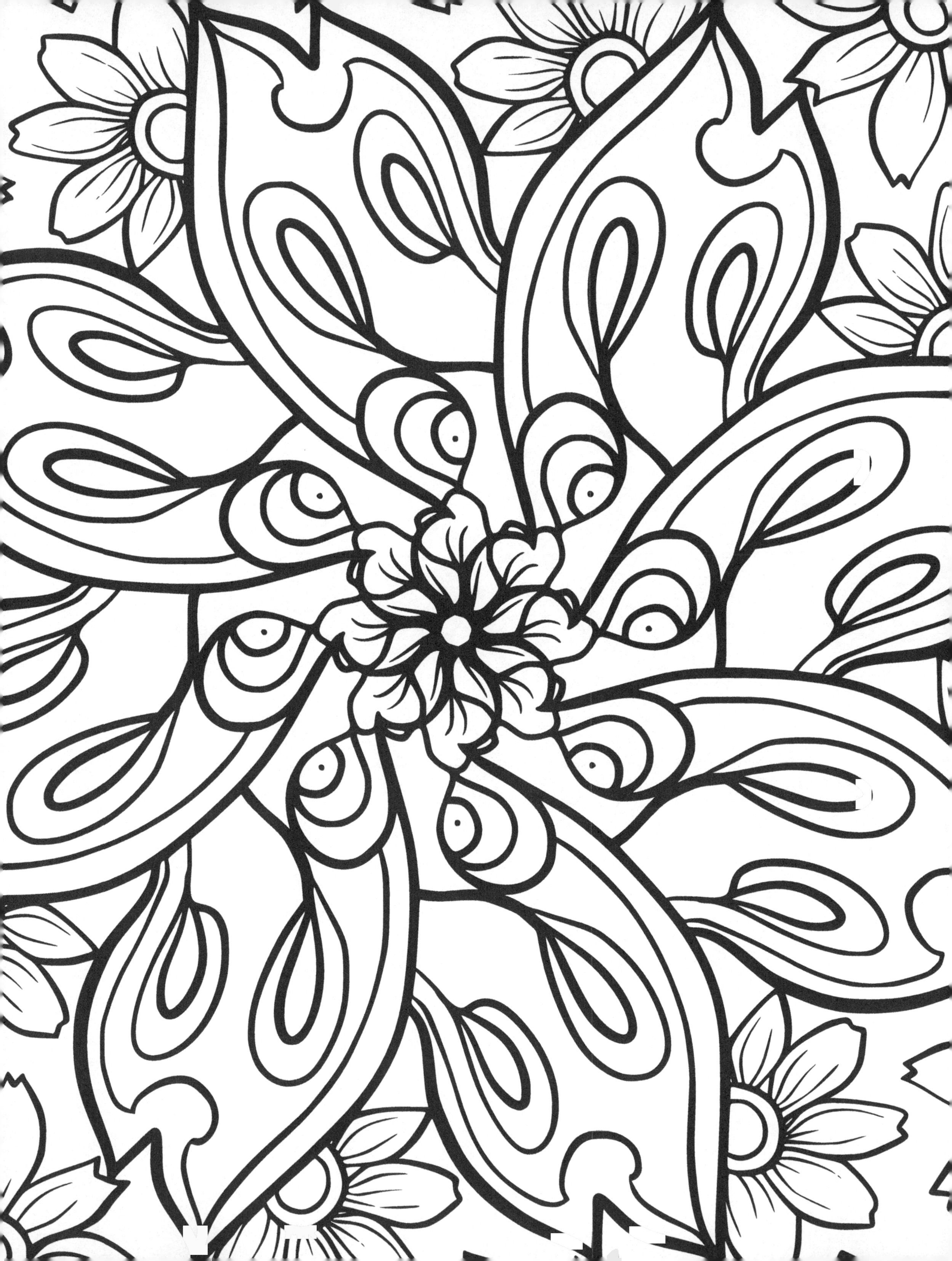

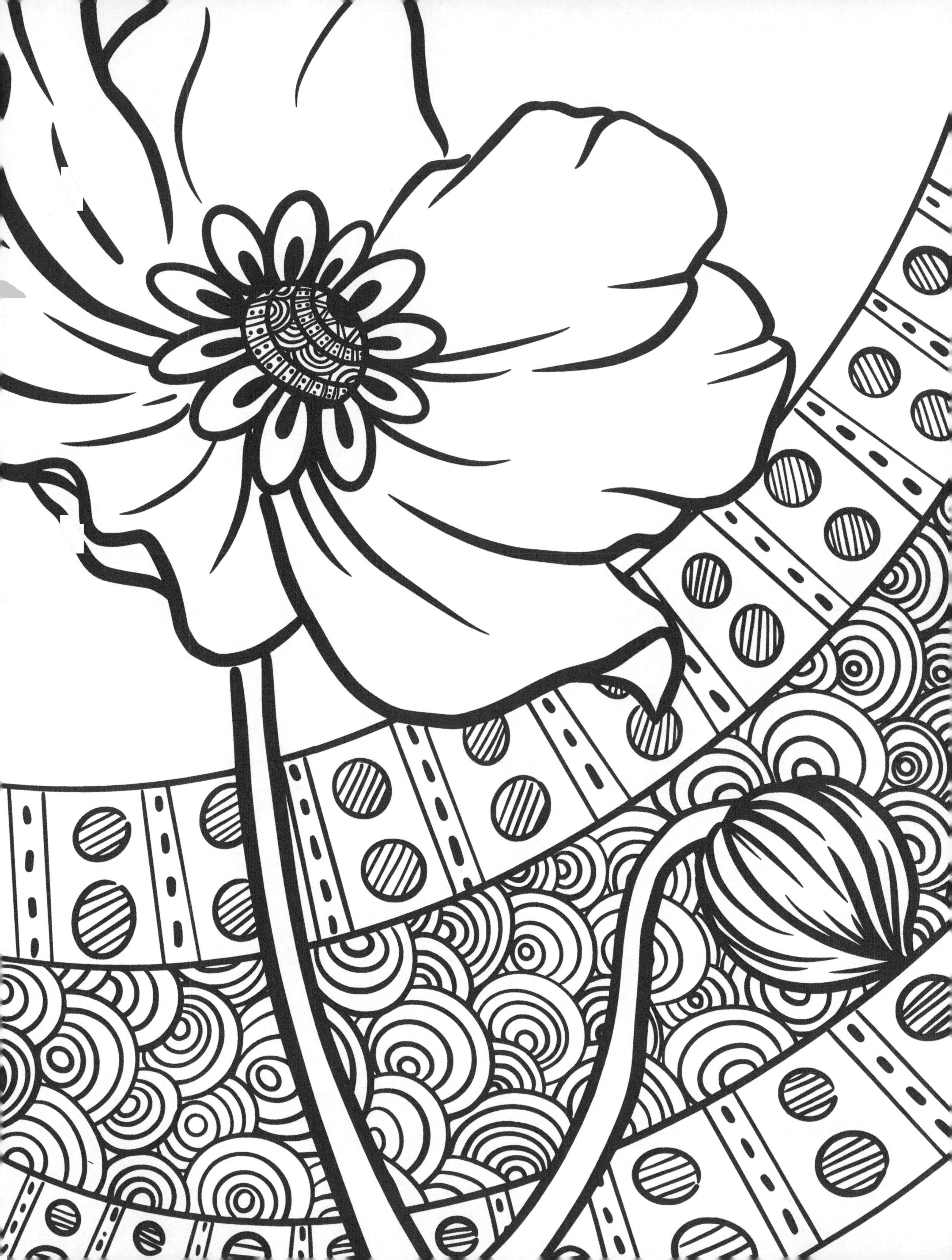

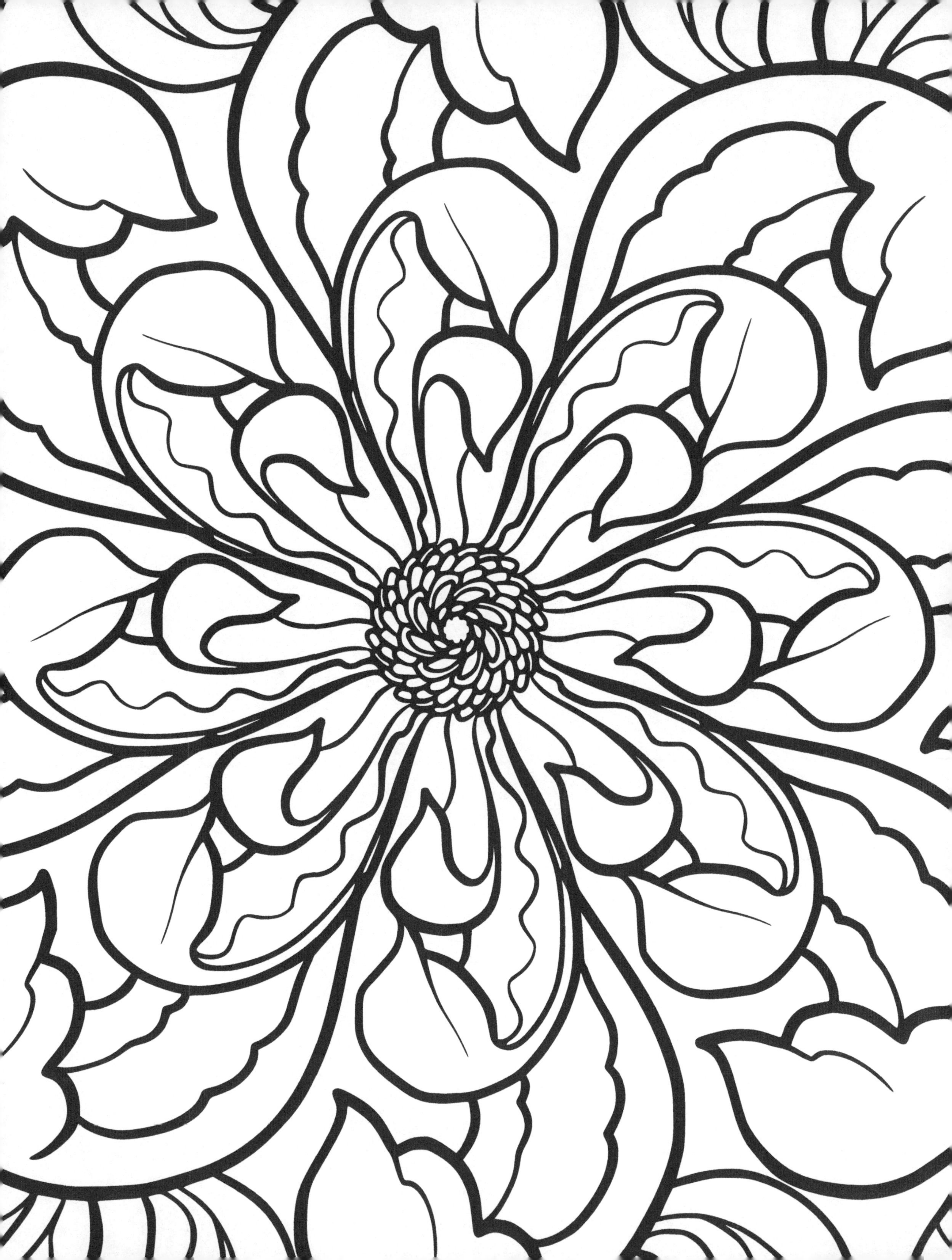

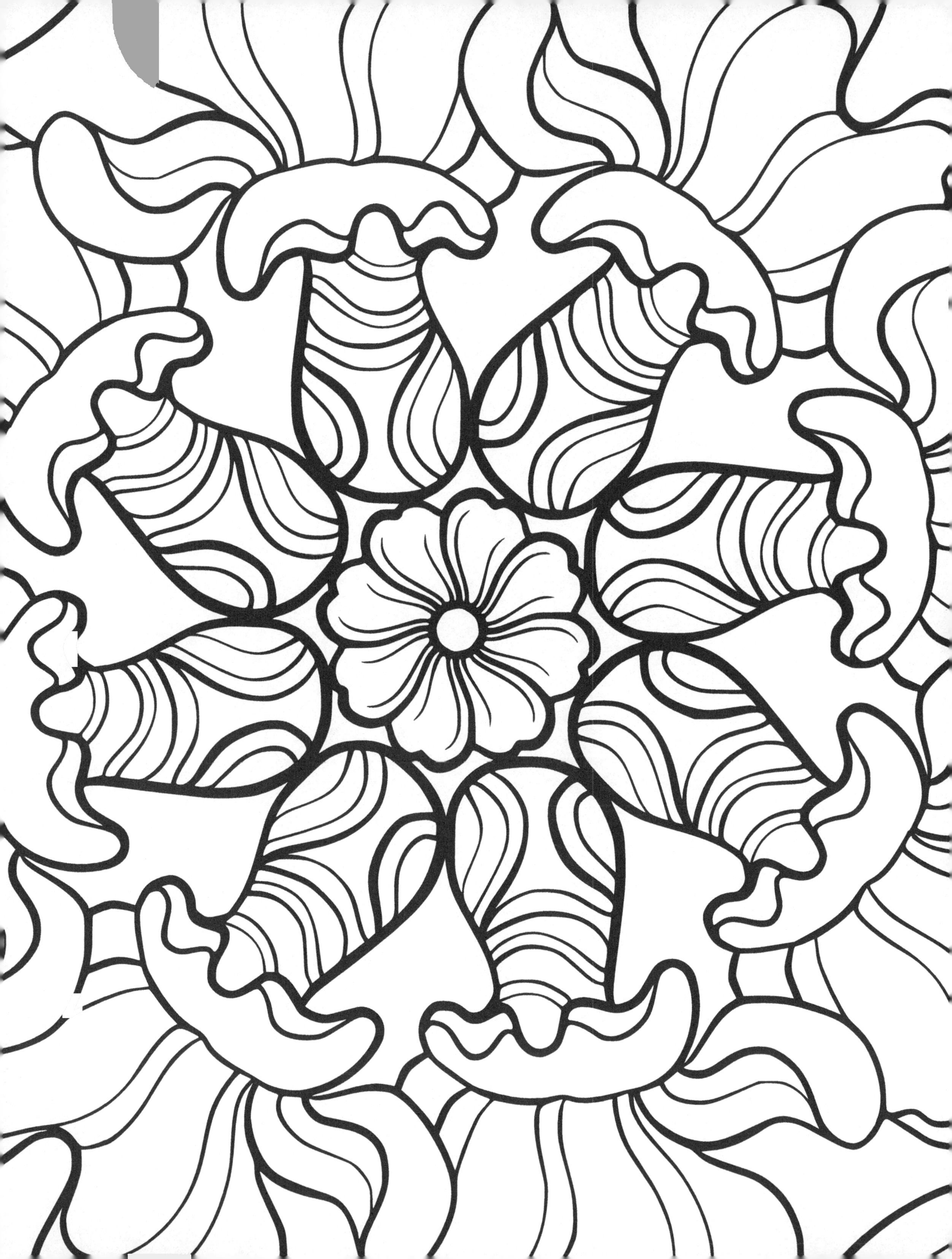

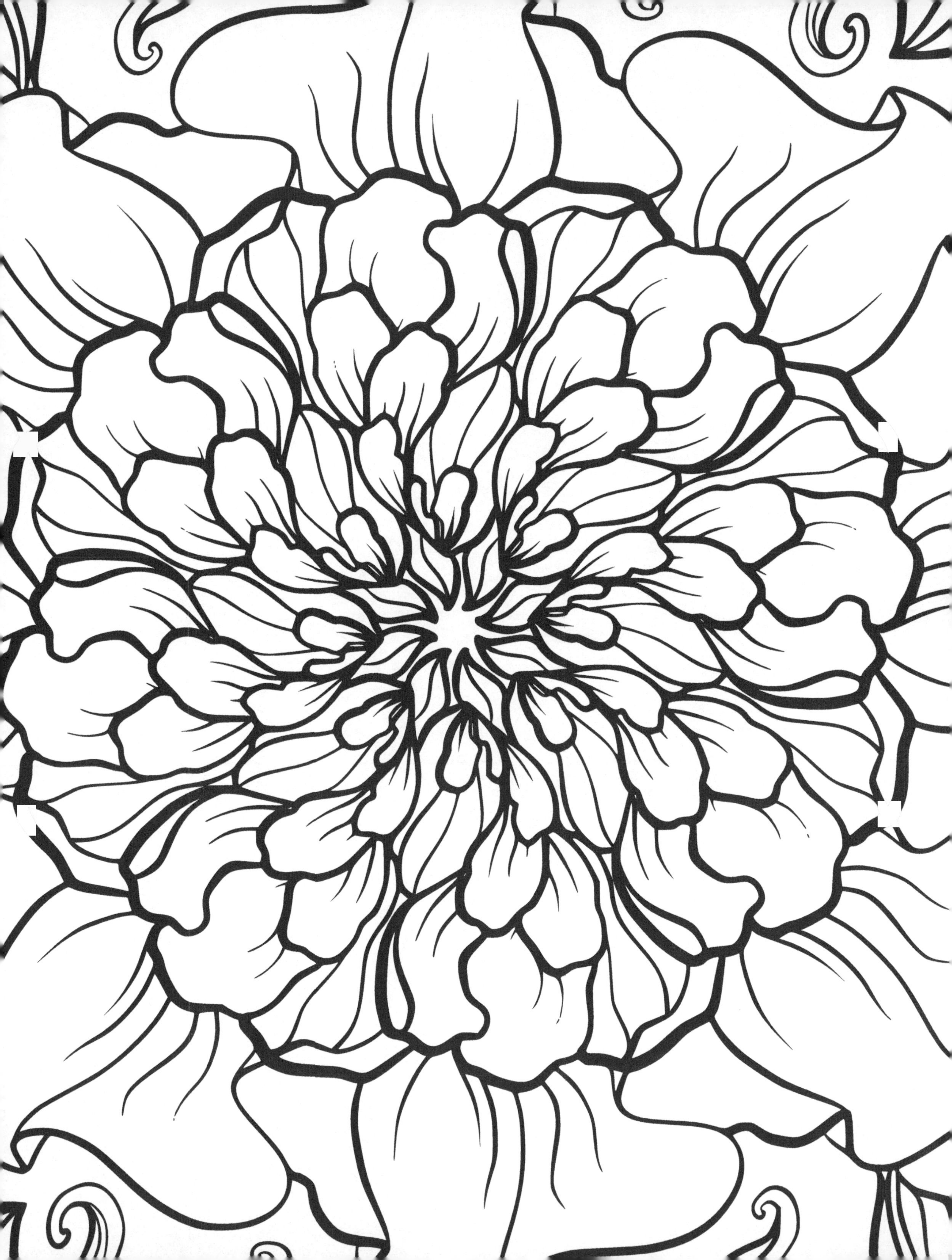

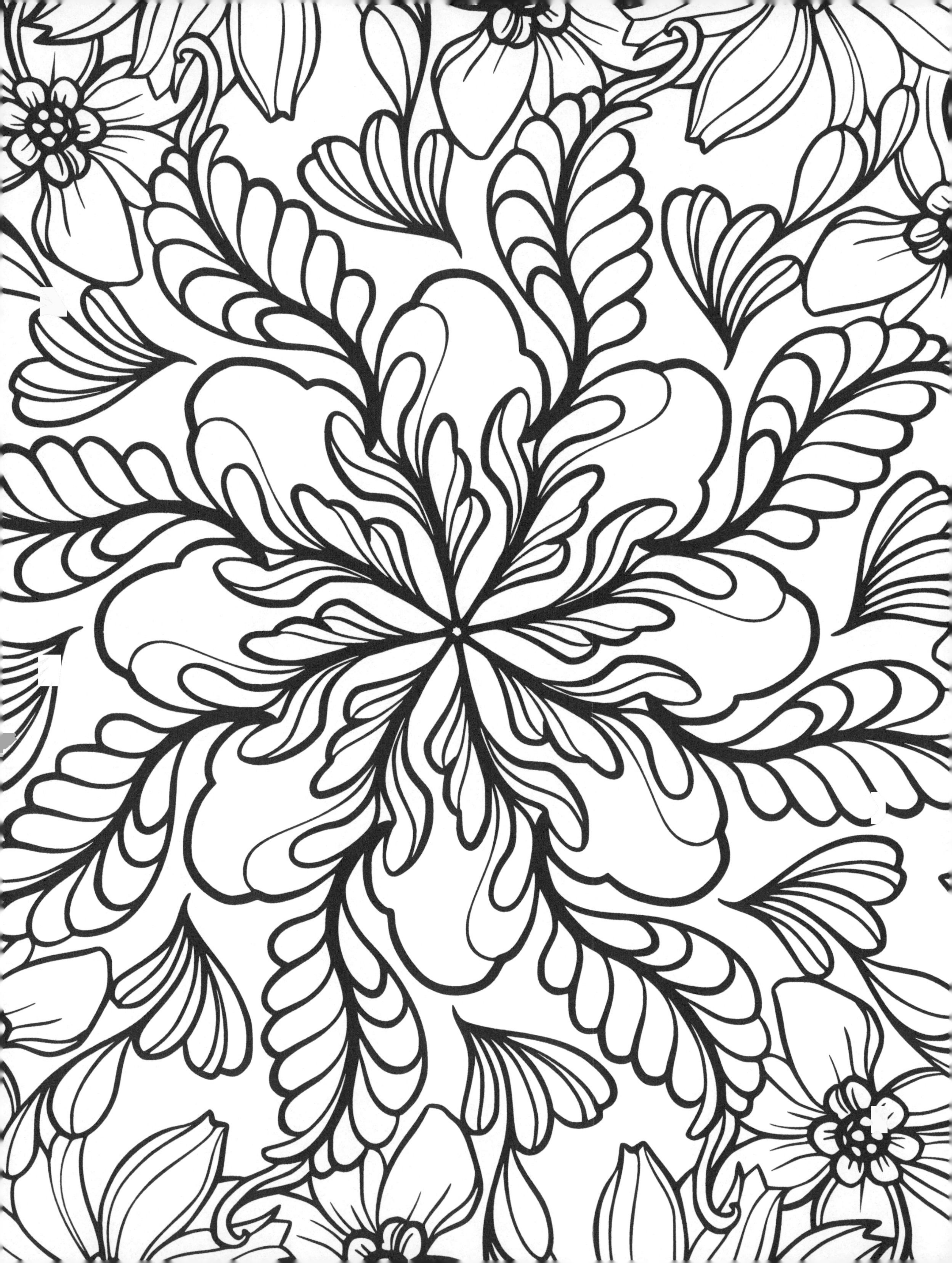

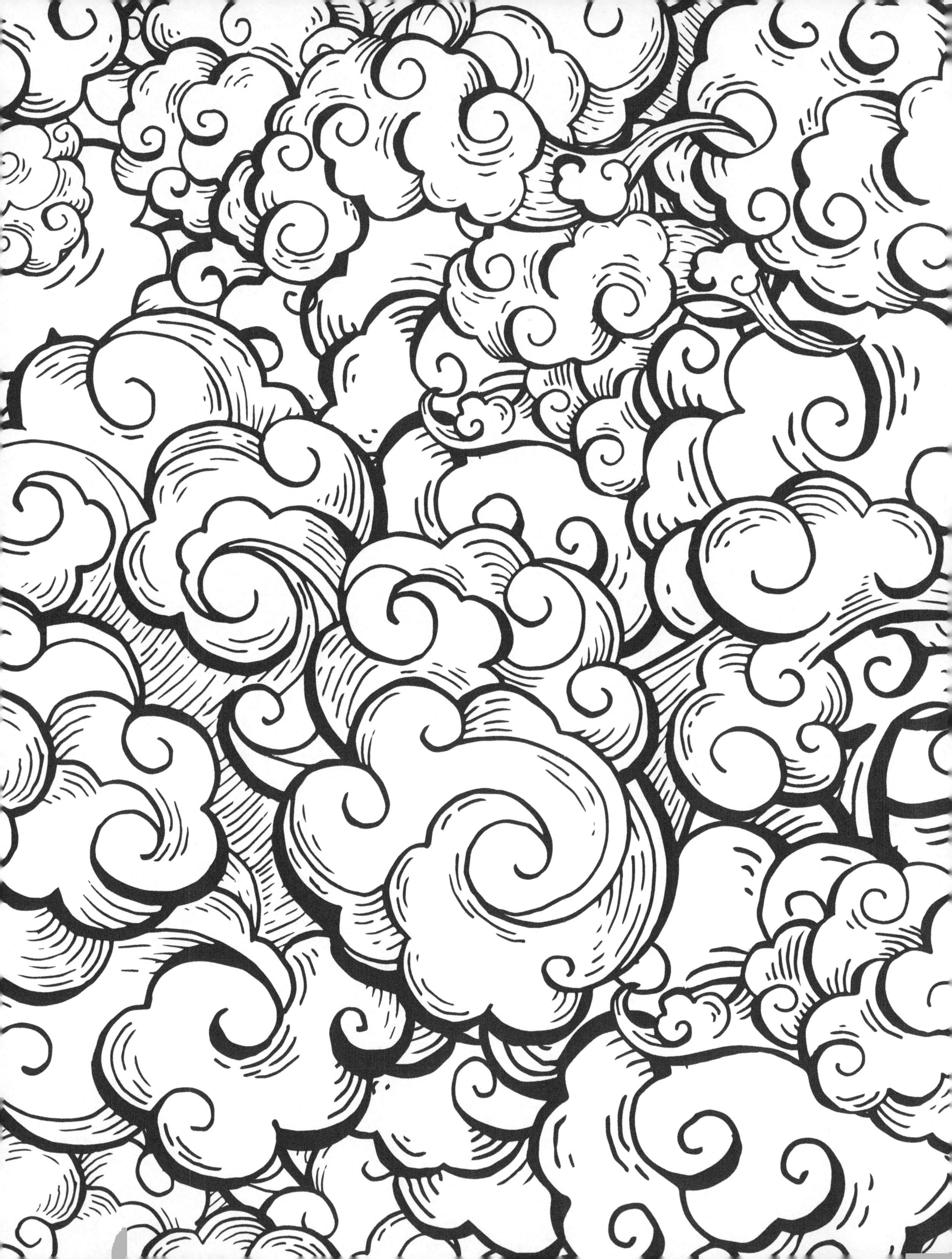

Made in the USA
Monee, IL
28 April 2023

32643598R00063